PSYCHOLOGY
for Busy People

Also by Joel Levy

Freudian Slips
Why We Do the Things We Do

PSYCHOLOGY
for Busy People

EVERYTHING YOU
NEED TO KNOW

Joel Levy

Michael O'Mara Books Limited

For my father

First published in Great Britain in 2019 by
Michael O'Mara Books Limited
9 Lion Yard
Tremadoc Road
London SW4 7NQ

A CIP catalogue record for this book is available from the British Library.

Papers used by Michael O'Mara Books Limited are natural, recyclable products
made from wood grown in sustainable forests. The manufacturing processes
conform to the environmental regulations of the country of origin.

ISBN: 978-1-78929-100-1 in hardback print format
ISBN: 978-1-78929-440-8 in paperback print format
ISBN: 978-1-78929-101-8 in ebook format

2 3 4 5 6 7 8 9 10

Designed and typeset by Design 23

Printed and bound by CPI Group (UK) Ltd, Croydon CR0 4YY

www.mombooks.com

CONTENTS

Introduction

WHAT IS PSYCHOLOGY?

Psychology is the study of the mind, but this simple formulation covers a dazzling and enormous field of human thought and behaviour, from the biology of the brain and nervous system to the meaning of love and happiness. Psychology has been called 'the science of humankind' because it tries to achieve a scientific study of the things that make us human. The key word here is 'science'; many other disciplines, such as philosophy, history and cultural studies, explore similar or overlapping fields, but psychology is different because it tries to approach them in a scientific fashion.

Science in this sense refers to a specific philosophy and methodology of knowledge and finding out. It involves using observations of phenomena (such as thoughts and behaviours) to formulate hypotheses, which are models or theories of how and why something happens. These hypotheses generate predictions that can be tested through experiments, and the degree to which the experimental results match up with the predictions confirms or invalidates the hypotheses. This at least is how science is supposed to work, and thus how psychology is supposed to work but, as you will learn, psychology is not always so straightforward.

Psychology is a massive and sprawling field and there are many ways in which it can be categorized, classified and divided. For instance, there is a difference between theoretical and applied psychology; the former explores the theories and first principles of psychological processes, while the latter seeks to apply psychological science to the real world, e.g. in treatment of mental illness.

This book broadly follows the typical textbook division of psychology, covering the following areas:

- Biological psychology – the study of the anatomy and physiology of the brain and nervous system.

- Cognitive psychology – the study of thinking, memory and emotion.

- Interpersonal psychology – how people relate to one another.

- Differential psychology – the ways in which people differ from each other, including personality and intelligence.

- Social psychology – the psychology of groups.

- Developmental psychology – how people grow, change and learn.

- Optimal or positive psychology – the psychology of happiness and well-being.

- Abnormal psychology – the study of mental disorders and how to treat them.

1

What you need to know about

THE BRAIN AND MIND

THE BRAIN AND THE NERVOUS SYSTEM

To understand psychology, first we have to explore the science behind it, specifically the science of the brain: the building blocks of the nervous system and the basic divisions of the nervous system; parts of the brain and how they correspond to different functions; key research and historical case studies that have revealed the fascinating and sometimes bizarre consequences of the link between structure and function; and some of the most mysterious aspects of this link, such as consciousness, sleep and hypnosis.

Neurons and the nervous system

The nervous system is divided into the 'central' and 'peripheral'. The central nervous system includes the brain and spinal cord, while the peripheral includes the nerves that extend to your skin and muscles, and which carry sensory and motor signals, or impulses.

Both the central and peripheral nervous systems are made up of nerve cells or neurons. In its most common form, a neuron consists of a cell body with many 'projections' leading away from it. Most of these projections are 'dendrites', which collect information from other neurons and bring it to the cell body. One of them, much longer than the others, is the axon, which can stretch up to 1 metre (3.3 feet) before branching to make contact with the dendrites of other neurons. In most neurons the axon is coated with a fatty white sheath called 'myelin', which acts as a kind of insulator, speeding the transmission of nervous signals.

Autonomic nervous system

In your body there is a whole system of nerves that is not under your conscious control. This is known as the autonomic nervous system, and it regulates aspects such as breathing, intestinal contractions, the relaxation and constriction of blood vessels, sweating and hair standing on end.

Signal processors and synapses

The neuron is like a tiny, electrically charged, biological microprocessor chip. It collects inputs from other neurons (via the dendrites), processes them (in the cell body) and gives an output (via the axon). By transporting ions across its cell membrane it builds up an electrical potential between the inside and the outside. If it receives enough inputs, a change in the cell membrane is triggered, causing rapid discharge of the electrical potential along its entire length. This produces a travelling electrical impulse known as a nervous signal. What happens next?

- Nervous signals (the inputs and outputs of neuron function) are transmitted between neurons at a synapse (where the axon of one neuron connects to the dendrite of another, separated only by a tiny synaptic gap).

- When a nerve signal arrives at the end of the axon, small packets of special chemicals known as neurotransmitters are released into the gap and picked up by receptor proteins on the other side.

- If enough of these signals are picked up at this dendrite and others belonging to the receiving neuron, it generates its own electrical impulse and distributes the nervous signal.

Different transmitters are used by different types of neuron, or in different areas of the brain, or they may have differing effects on the same neuron – some will excite the neuron, others will inhibit it, making it less likely to fire. Neurotransmitters play a vital role in controlling brain processes. By altering the subtle balance of neurotransmitters in the brain (by using pharmaceutical or recreational drugs, for instance), it is possible to affect mood, motor control, perception, memory and even consciousness itself.

For example, the neurotransmitter 'serotonin' plays a major role in the production and regulation of emotions and mood. Serotonin levels change over the course of the day and the year, can be affected by the food you eat and are modified by antidepressants like Prozac and drugs like Ecstasy.

Breaking down the brain

The central nervous system includes the spine, the brainstem, the cerebellum and the cerebrum:

- The spine collects nervous impulses from 'sensory' and 'feedback' neurons in the peripheral nervous system and distributes signals to them. Some neurological functions, such as the knee-jerk reflex exhibited when a hammer strikes the fleshy part just below the knee, are executed entirely within the spine, but most depend on signals going to and from the brain. The spine comes up through the base of the skull and swells into the most primitive part of the brain, the brainstem.

• The brainstem controls the unconscious processes of the body, e.g. breathing and whether you are awake or asleep. All nerve signals between the brain and the body and senses, incoming and outgoing, pass through this region, and it is also where nerve signals from the right-hand side of your body cross over to lead to the left-hand side of the brain, and vice versa.

• The cerebellum sits at the base of the brain and controls the complex programmes of neuronal firing needed to produce smooth, coordinated and balanced movement. For example, while you may consciously decide to walk using higher parts of your brain, it is the cerebellum that actually carries out the neural processes involved.

• The cerebrum is what most people mean when they talk about the brain. This is where all your higher mental functions like thinking, memory and language reside, and it is also the seat of consciousness. The outer surface of the cerebrum, the cerebral cortex, is deeply wrinkled and fissured so that it looks like a walnut. This extensive wrinkling allows more of the brain's surface layers to be packed into the skull.

- Between the cerebrum and lower parts of the brain are 'in-between' structures that link the conscious processes of the cerebrum to the unconscious processes of the brainstem: the thalamus, hypothalamus and limbic system. They are involved in generating and regulating the 'animal' parts of your personality – your emotions, fears and basic drives, such as hunger, thirst and sexual desire. They are also involved in learning and memory formation.

Right-brain, left-brain

The cerebrum is divided into two halves, known as the left and right cerebral hemispheres. Although the two are ana-tomically almost identical, and often work in concert, there are some differences between their roles. In most people the left hemisphere is dominant for functions such as language, logic and mathematical ability, while the right is dominant for emotions, art and spatial reasoning. Each hemisphere controls the sensory and motor functions of the opposite side of the body, but in most people the left hemisphere is dominant for motor control, making them right-handed.

We are not normally conscious of any of this separation of roles, thanks to the corpus callosum, a bridge of neural fibres that connects the two hemispheres providing a high-speed information transfer link. Messages pass so quickly between the hemispheres that they are able to operate as a single unit.

Unilateral neglect – getting half the story

Occasionally, through stroke, injury or surgery, one hemisphere of the brain is damaged while the other continues to function normally. People afflicted in this way can display a condition known as unilateral neglect, where they appear to be unable to perceive or think about one side of space. Symptoms include putting all the numbers in one half when drawing a clock face; shaving only half the face; eating only half of the food on a plate, even though hungry (if the plate is turned round, the subject is then able to eat the other half); and even failing to recognize limbs on the affected side.

Lobes of the brain

Each cerebral hemisphere is divided into four lobes: frontal, temporal, parietal and occipital.

- The frontal lobes (which deal with the most 'intellectual' functions, such as planning, forethought, strategy, will and self-control) are at the front of the brain. They also contain the main site of voluntary muscle control, the motor cortex, and some language control areas.

- The temporal lobes (which are involved in hearing, smell and making sense of language) are on either side of the brain. Disturbances (such as epilepsy) of this part of the brain are linked to frightening sensations such as feeling menacing presences or hearing preternatural sounds.

- The parietal lobes (containing the main area of sensory cortex, where sensations from different parts of the body are consciously felt) are across the top of the brain.

- The occipital lobes (which are mainly concerned with vision) are at the back of the brain.

An important question is, how do we know what different parts of the brain do? Locating brain function on brain structures is one of the primary preoccupations of neuropsychology, the branch of psychology concerned with the nervous system and the relation between brain structure and function. Today researchers use advanced brain scanning and imaging technology to look at the brains of living people after or during various types of thinking. In the past, however, researchers had to examine brains post-mortem and link what they saw with the person's clinical history. A celebrated early example of this was Phineas Gage (see page 20), who survived having a metal rod blasted through his brain.

Some parts of the brain are named after the neurologists who linked damage in these regions to specific deficits in their patients. For instance, Carl Wernicke (1848–1905), a German physician and psychiatrist, found that patients who suffer damage (e.g. through a stroke) to a brain structure – now known as Wernicke's area – can lose the ability to link language with meaning. This produces a characteristic 'word salad' (a jumble of sounds that resembles language but has no meaning). Damage to another brain structure, named after the French physician Paul Broca, (1824–80) was linked by him to an opposing syndrome in which the individual understands language but cannot produce the movements involved in speech.

Other areas where function can be localized (or mapped) closely to the brain's structure include the 'motor cortex' and the 'somatosensory cortex'. These are strips of the cortex near the border between the frontal and parietal lobes. Different parts of these strips govern motor control/ sensation in specific parts of the body, so that it is possible to map a direct relationship between parts of the body and spots on the surface of the brain. However, many – perhaps most – cognitive functions do not map quite so neatly onto distinct parts of the brain; these functions are said to be 'distributed' because the apparatus that mediates them is spread around through the brain.

Mapping the brain

Phineas Gage (1823–60) was a railroad foreman who, in 1848, was caught in an explosion which blasted an iron rod through his head. The doctor who treated him, John Harlow, claimed that the accident had radically altered Gage's personality, changing him from a dependable, conscientious fellow of 'well-balanced mind' into a foul-mouthed, impulsive drunk: 'the balance between his intellectual faculties and animal propensities seems to have been destroyed'.

Harlow linked the change to the nature of the brain damage to his frontal lobes, and the case became a touchstone for the effort to equate a brain function to a specific area. Harlow's report seemed to demonstrate that the frontal lobes controlled what are now called 'executive capacities': planning, foresight, self-control and the inhibition of 'animal instincts'.

Gage's case may not be able to bear the weight of interpretation that has been laid on it, since the exact nature of his brain damage has been difficult to prove. Nonetheless, Gage is still cited in textbooks, and has proved an important figure in the evolution of psychology as it developed its central, materialist thesis proposing that the mind is a biological phenomenon that maps directly onto the brain.

CONSCIOUSNESS, SLEEP, DREAMS AND HYPNOSIS

Human consciousness involves awareness, subjectivity and self-awareness, but its precise meaning depends on the context in which it is discussed. Such contexts range from the physiological, as with the distinction between coma, sleep and wakefulness, to the philosophical, and the distinction between human and animal or machine consciousness.

Within each of these contexts there are often different definitions, levels and types of consciousness. To give just one example, in 1998 the American philosopher Ned Block (b. 1942) drew a distinction between 'phenomenal consciousness' (direct experience of a phenomenon) and 'access consciousness' (direct experience to which a person has conscious access – i.e. is paying attention to). These often coincide, but not always, as in the example of someone who becomes aware that the clock is chiming only belatedly, but who is then able to say how many chimes have already sounded.

Arousal and alertness

Perhaps the easiest version of consciousness to understand is the difference between being awake, asleep or knocked out, whether by anaesthesia or a blow to the head. Someone who is under anaesthesia is clearly unconscious, but what about someone who is asleep? Neuropsychologists describe

the difference as one of 'arousal', in the sense of the physiological measures of brain and body activity. These measures
include heart and breathing rate, and electrical activity in
the brain as measured by an electroencephalogram (EEG).
Another term for arousal in this sense is 'alertness'.

There are two main types of alertness: 'phasic' and 'tonic':

- Phasic is short-term alertness, such as the heightened
  awareness, focus and bodily responses you might
  experience on spotting an approaching threat.

- The alertness or arousal serves to orient the
  consciousness towards important and novel stimuli.
  If the stimulus persists or repeats continuously, you
  habituate, or become used to it, and phasic alertness
  subsides. This helps to avoid wasting physical and
  mental energy on a constant stimulus, enabling you
  to conserve energy for potential new stimuli.

- Tonic alertness describes the gradual change in
  internal arousal, as occurs over the course of a day, as
  you move from sleep to wakefulness and go through
  periods of drowsiness or otherwise lowered arousal.

- This kind of alertness is controlled primarily by
  electrical activity in a part of the brainstem known as
  the 'reticular activating system' (RAS). If the brainstem

of an animal is severed below the RAS, it will be paralyzed but can remain alert, and sleep and wake as normal. If the brainstem is severed above the RAS, the animal will fall into a continuous deep sleep.

Sleep

Sleep is a distinct state in which consciousness is suspended and a person is mostly, but not completely, unresponsive to the outside world. It is different from resting, because during sleep the muscles are relaxed and the metabolic rate is reduced, while measures of brain activity, such as EEGs, show characteristic changes. Sleep psychologists talk about five stages of sleep: one stage known as 'rapid eye movement' (REM) sleep, and four of 'non-REM' (NREM) sleep. Typically, you will move through these stages in the following order:

- Transition from wakefulness to sleep: also known as the 'hypnagogic period', when the pattern of electrical activity in your brain changes after you shut your eyes. Brain electrical activity comes in cycles (brain waves), and these cycles change from relatively high frequency (beta waves) to lower frequency (alpha waves), which are characteristic of the relaxed mind.

- Stage I NREM: alpha waves are replaced by low frequency theta waves; the eyes roll slowly; heart rate slows and muscles begin to relax. You are easily woken from this stage.

- Stage II NREM: brain activity shows one- to two-second-long bursts of activity known as 'sleep spindles' from the pattern they make on an EEG readout. It is still easy to wake you from this stage.

- Stage III NREM: very low-frequency delta waves appear, your blood pressure, body temperature and heart rate fall, and you will be unresponsive to external stimulation and hard to wake.

- Stage IV NREM: delta waves dominate brain activity as you enter deep or delta sleep. It takes about half an hour to reach this stage, and you spend about half an hour in deep sleep, from which it's hard to wake. Gradually you cycle back up through the stages, but instead of re-entering stage I, you will move into a new phase, REM sleep.

- REM sleep: also known as 'active sleep', when the brain is as active as during wakefulness and the eyes move around but the rest of the body is paralyzed. Heart and breathing rate and blood pressure increase, so that physiologically you appear to be highly active, yet it would be very hard to wake you. This stage is also known as 'paradoxical sleep'. Most dreaming occurs during REM sleep.

The functions of these various stages, and of sleep in general, remain open to question. No single theory fits all the facts. For instance, if sleep is just about saving energy, why have an REM stage that uses up as much energy as being awake?

Lurkers on the threshold

The periods of transition in and out of wakefulness are known respectively as the 'hypnagogic' and 'hypnopompic'. These states are associated with strange sensations, perceptions and hallucinations, such as sensing the presence of unknown and often malevolent entities, or hearing voices. This may be related to increased brain activity in the temporal lobes, parts of the cortex known to be associated with such perceptions. Perhaps not coincidentally the peak incidence of paranormal experience is at times when people are likely to be falling asleep or waking up.

Dreams

Although psychologists know something about *how* people dream, explaining *why* they dream is much harder. So what can we say?

- Adults typically have four to six dreams a night, each lasting from five to thirty minutes.

- Children under ten actually have fewer dreams than adults.

- Furthermore, only a tiny fraction of dreams are recalled, but we do know that dreams commonly have strong emotional content, most often related to negative emotions such as anxiety.

- Most dreams occur during REM sleep, when the body is expending a lot of energy, which implies that dreaming must have some benefit in evolutionary terms, and this is reinforced by a phenomenon called…

- 'REM rebound', when people or animals deliberately deprived of REM sleep seem to develop an REM deficit, which they make up for by spending more time in REM sleep on the next occasion they are able to sleep.

- REM sleep, and presumably the dreaming that is such a notable feature of it, is evidently an especially important component of sleep. However, pinning down its function and benefits has proved very difficult.

In ancient times, a major function imputed to dreams was healing, and similar beliefs still hold true today, including among many psychologists. In psychoanalysis, for instance, following on from the view of Sigmund Freud (1856–1939) that dreams are the 'royal road to the unconscious' (meaning one of the best available insights into the mechanics of the unconscious mind), dreams are seen as a kind of psychic sandbox. In dreams, Freud argued, repressed fears and desires, and other contents of the unconscious, are allowed to emerge and play themselves out. This process is important, psychoanalysts believe, as it allows conflicts and anxieties to be explored and resolved. However, as so few dreams can be remembered, it might seem that their use as agents of psychic healthcare is limited.

The psychological approach known as 'cognitive psychology', which views mental processes as more akin to computer processes, points to evidence that dreaming (along with sleep in general) enhances learning and memory. Cognitive theories about dreaming include the role of dreams in rehearsing and integrating knowledge and memories, and also in 'cleaning out' obsolete and defunct memories.

Hypnosis

The term hypnosis comes from the Greek '*hypnos*', meaning 'sleep', reflecting the early days of research into this phenomenon when it was known as 'somnambulism' ('sleepwalking'). This was the term used by the Marquis de Puységur (1751–1825), a follower of the Viennese physician Anton Mesmer (1734–1815), who was able to induce altered states of consciousness in people, in a phenomenon widely known as 'mesmerism', although Mesmer himself attributed his 'powers' to a physical force he called 'animal magnetism'.

Puységur was particularly interested in what was known as 'magnetic sleep', a kind of side-effect of mesmerism, in which people acted like sleepwalkers: passive, suggestible and in a kind of trance. His research on somnambulism was later taken up by the Scottish physician James Braid (1795–1860), who coined the term 'hypnosis' and definitively shifted the phenomenon from the physical to the psychological realm.

Hypnosis seems to offer access to a distinct and different state or type of consciousness. Freud tried to use it as a tool in psychoanalysis, and many claims have been made for the power of hypnosis in boosting recall, controlling behaviour, resolving psychological problems and enhancing mind–body interactions (e.g. allowing mental control of blood pressure, circulation and pain reception). Yet the fundamentals of hypnosis remain controversial: there are two opposing schools of thought that emerged in late nineteenth-century France, and which remain unresolved today:

- The pioneering psychiatrist Pierre Janet (1859–1947) proposed that hypnosis induces a special state involving some degree of dissociation of consciousness, with some parts of the mind or personality 'going to sleep' while others continue to function. This is still the popular view of hypnosis, but it was challenged almost from the start by …

- Hippolyte Bernheim (1840–1919), a professor of medicine in Nancy, who argued that hypnosis is not special, but merely a normal psychological process involving suggestion and suggestibility. This 'non-state' theory of hypnosis has developed into a view of hypnosis as a kind of tacit role play between the hypnotizer and the hypnotized (who may be the same individual).

Research has also dispelled many popular beliefs about hypnosis. It cannot improve recall and its use in 'recovering' memories is false and potentially dangerous. People cannot be hypnotized against their will, and the hypnotic subject is not under the control of the hypnotist.

The emotions

Brain structures are often described in terms of their evolutionary 'level', with the deeper and lower structures such as the limbic system and brainstem seen as 'primitive' or 'animal' parts of the brain. Similarly, the functions of these brain structures are placed lower in the cognitive hierarchy, with instincts, drives and emotions said to be the animal or primitive parts of our psychology.

The sensory organs feed information about the outside world to the brain, and the initial processing of this sensory stimulus takes place in brain structures such as the thalamus. This is where particularly notable, striking and potentially important (dangerous or beneficial) stimuli are 'rated' for salience (flagged up for notice and action). The thalamus links to the 'amygdala' (a small, almond-shaped organ of the brain that sits on top of the brainstem) and from there to the cortex. In the cortex, higher-level processing works out the fine details of the sensory input, but by this time emotional responses have already been set in motion.

What are these responses? Emotions have three components:

• Subjective experience, including feelings, thoughts and memories.

- Visceral states, i.e. physiological changes involving the autonomic nervous system, and the endocrine system, which regulates hormones.

- Associated behaviours.

But in what order do these elements occur, and which are causes and which effects?

How many emotions are there?

Since the start of psychology as a science, psychologists have tried to categorize and enumerate the emotions. One of the most influential efforts has been the work of the American psychologist Paul Ekman (b. 1934), who made cross-cultural studies of recognition of and responses to photographs of facial expressions. He identified six primary emotions: happiness, disgust, surprise, sadness, anger and fear. Another American psychologist, Robert Plutchik (1927–2006), drew up an emotion wheel that arranged four pairs of opposing primary emotions: joy/sorrow; disgust/acceptance; fear/anger; surprise/ anticipation in a wheel, with more complex secondary emotions radiating out.

Are we happy because we are smiling?

The commonsense view of emotion is that something makes us happy, sad or angry, and then our bodies respond appropriately: in other words, psychological states trigger physiological, bodily responses. But two psychology pioneers – the American psychologist and philosopher Willam James (1842–1910) and the Danish physician Carl Lange (1834–1900) – independently proposed a theory that turned this approach on its head. What is now known as the 'James–Lange theory' argues that the subjective sensation of emotion actually follows on from physiology and behaviour. Our higher faculties interpret instinctive bodily responses only *after* the fact or, as James put it: 'We feel sorry because we cry, angry because we strike, afraid because we tremble.'

Critics pointed out that the James–Lange theory only works if there are specific and distinct patterns of physiological arousal for each emotional state. In practice this is not the case: patterns of physiological arousal are broadly similar between different emotional states. For instance, both anger and fear are associated with increased heart rate and blood pressure, dilation of pupils, faster breathing and increased blood flow to the muscles. In 1962 the American psychologist Stanley Schachter (1992–97) came up with a cognitive labelling theory, proposing that, while physiological arousal is the starting point for experience of emotion, the actual nature of that emotion depends on how this arousal is labelled.

2

What you need to know about
MEMORY AND THINKING

Thought, memory and language are all forms of what psychologists call 'cognition'. It may seem obvious that cognition should be the main concern of psychology, but in some ways cognition poses an existential threat to psychology's claim to be the scientific study of the mind. How can we ever truly know what goes on inside someone else's head? Can we really understand even our own thought processes?

STUDYING THE INNER MIND

The birth of psychology as an independent science occurred in 1879 when the German physician Wilhelm Wundt (1832–1920) opened the Institute for Experimental Psychology at the University of Leipzig. Wundt's answer to the challenge of 'subjectivity', i.e. the impossibility of objectively observing another's thinking, was 'introspection', a technique by which an individual attempts to report objectively on his or her own thought processes.

Wundt believed that a sufficiently scientific mind could be trained to become a dispassionate and scientifically precise observer of its own inner workings. The essential fallacy of this approach provoked a violent reaction, led by the American psychologist John B Watson (1878–1958) in his 1913 manifesto 'Psychology as the Behaviourist Views It'.

Watson argued that the internal workings of the mind could not be scientifically studied. The only valid study must be of what is observable, namely behaviour; this school of psychology became known as 'behaviourism'. For several decades this remained the dominant school of thought, but very early on some researchers pointed to evidence that proved it is possible to have insight into cognition. From these seeds developed what is known as 'cognitive psychology'. The approach of cognitive psychology is to combine clever, experimental methods with an information-processing model. This model, based on the concepts of computer science that emerged from the 1940s onward, sees the mind as a processing unit, which operates on inputs (such as perceptual stimuli or memories) to generate outputs (cognitions and behaviours).

Little Albert

Behaviourism was criticized for being more like dogma than science, a point illustrated by one of the more notorious episodes in the history of psychological research. John B. Watson's best-known experiment was his 'Little Albert' study of conditioning, inspired by the Russian scientist Ivan Pavlov (1849–1936) and his experiment showing that dogs could be conditioned (trained or taught) so that a stimulus, such as ringing a bell, could make them salivate. Watson wanted to show that the same process could be applied to humans, and in what would now be regarded as an ethically dubious experiment he set out to condition a nine-month old infant, Albert B., widely known as 'Little Albert'.

Watson claimed to have conditioned Albert to associate a white rat with a nasty shock (a loud noise), so that the poor child responded with distress at the mere sight of a rat or to anything else white and furry, including a rabbit, a Santa Claus hat and even Watson's beard. It later transpired that Little Albert was actually Douglas Merritte, who suffered from cognitive impairment due to hydrocephalus, from which he died at the age of six. It seemed likely that Watson had chosen Douglas because the boy was less likely to show a prior response to stimuli such as a rat, a confounding variable that invalidated the study. Watson went on to build much of his later career on the back of the Little Albert study, despite knowing that it was flawed.

Paying attention

The most immediate and evident manifestation of cognition – and of consciousness itself – is what you are thinking about or focusing on in any given moment. Attention is the core of 'consciousness', indeed it is the term widely used by cognitive psychologists as a stand-in for the wider, and often less tractable, concept of consciousness.

Shadowing

In 1953 the acoustic engineer Colin Cherry (1914–79) designed an ingenious experiment to explore how people attend to what they hear, and what happens when there are multiple streams or channels of incoming information. This was of great practical interest in professions such as air traffic control, where a controller needs to filter out irrelevant sound/speech and focus only on the most important – or salient – information. In the experiment:

- Cherry's subjects wore headphones with different auditory inputs for each ear. He asked them to attend to only one of these and, to ensure that they focused all their attention on the one channel, the subjects were asked to 'shadow' the speech they heard by repeating it aloud.

- Later they were tested to see what, if anything, they had picked up from the track playing in the other ear.

- It turned out that people can report almost nothing from the unattended channel; although they can tell whether it consisted of words or just tones, and can report the gender of a speaker, they fail to notice what language was being spoken, whether messages were played backwards and even the repetition of single words.

In 1958 this kind of research prompted the British psychologist Donald Broadbent (1926–93) to construct a model of the cognitive processes involved. Using a flowchart with boxes and arrows, a conceptual paradigm that became central to cognitive psychology, Broadbent's flowchart shows multiple incoming channels of auditory information, with an attention 'module' acting as a filter to select the most salient, which then travels on to the cortex for higher-level processing.

In Broadbent's model all incoming channels except the most salient are blocked, but this meant that it failed to explain one of the best-known phenomena in the field, the one that had helped prompt Cherry's original research: the cocktail-party effect (in which people are able to filter out background noise to focus on one voice). Revisions of the model add extra stages of processing and partial filtering to accommodate the kind of pre- or subconscious attention that must be operating to explain the cocktail-party effect.

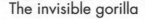

The invisible gorilla

In a 1959 experiment it was shown that almost a third of a cinema audience watching trailers before a movie failed to notice a man dressed as a ghost walking across the stage. In 1999 Daniel Simons and Christopher Chabris performed an updated version of this experiment, with a trial in which subjects were asked to watch a video of a basketball match and count passes between two players. With their attention focused on the specific task, about half of the subjects failed to notice someone in a gorilla suit walking across the court in the middle of the match. This 'invisible gorilla' appeared to demonstrate a phenomenon dubbed 'inattentional blindness', when things are only 'visible' to our conscious minds when we are attending to them.

MEMORY BASICS

Memory is the ability to retain learning and experience. It is one of the core, essential elements of the human psyche and the foundation stone of all human achievement. The British neurobiologist Colin Blakemore (b. 1944) pointed out that without memory 'there could be no language, no art, no science, no culture. Civilization itself is the distillation of human memory.'

Brain structures and memory

Memory involves both storage and recall, and most of the brain is involved at some point in these two processes. The important regions include:

- The thalamus, located on top of the brainstem, which acts as a node for early processing and the integration of incoming sensory stimuli. It is the first port of call for information arriving in the brain and it also integrates information from different sources, relaying it to the appropriate structures in the rest of the brain. As the gateway for incoming information from the senses, the thalamus probably plays an important role in the workings of the sensory register.

- The hippocampus is part of the limbic system and plays important roles in many different aspects of memory, such as training in new skills, learning new facts and recognizing faces and places. It is particularly important in the type of memory known as 'short-term' or 'working memory' (STM).

- The amygdala plays an important role in the generation of emotion, and in memory formation it helps to label memories with emotional content or significance.

The cerebral cortex is thought to be where memories are stored, although the specifics of this storage are likely to be highly complex and nuanced. Prior to the 1960s it was assumed that specific memories must be represented in the brain by specific networks of neurons in specific parts of the cortex, so that it would effectively be possible to cut the physical trace of a memory out of the cortex and thus delete that memory.

In the 1960s research was done on patients undergoing brain surgery. Each patient remained conscious during the operation, while the surface of the brain (the cortex) was exposed. By stimulating the cortex with tiny electrodes, surgeons could trigger memories but, to their surprise, they also found that the same memory could be triggered by stimulating widely different spots. This research developed the 'distributed processing model', which posits networks of neurons that represent memories confined not to one spot, but distributed across the cortex and other parts of the brain.

Pribram's holonomic brain theory

In 1969 the Austrian-American neurosurgeon and psychiatrist Karl Pribram (1919–2015) refined this theory with his 'holonomic' brain model, which views memories in the brain as being like holograms. In a hologram, the way that the original image is recorded is quite different to a normal photograph. In the latter each part of the photograph records the information for the equivalent part of the original image; if you cut a photo into four quarters each quarter will depict only the matching quarter of the original image. In a hologram, however, every point on the hologram's surface contains a record of the entire original image so that if you smash a hologram into pieces, each piece will still depict the whole of the original image, but with reduced clarity compared to the whole.

Pribram suggested that memory is stored in the brain in a similar way to how an image is stored in a hologram. So, a memory is stored across a whole area of the brain, and any part of this area can be used to reconstruct the original memory, although it requires the whole area to recall the memory with total clarity. Due to Pribram's suggestion that each memory is a different hologram (the brain thus containing multiple holographic regions), the model is said to be holonomic rather than just holographic.

Pribram's theory explains how losing parts of your brain, for instance through ageing or drinking, can result in a degradation of memory rather than a total loss, and why we sometimes remember scenes or episodes only vaguely, rather than simply remembering some parts of the scene not at all and some parts with full clarity. However, the opposite can also be true – you might remember virtually nothing about your first visit to the beach except for the taste of your first ice cream, which you can recall with total clarity. So Pribram's theory is not necessarily the whole story.

Memory modes

One of the most important and influential models of memory is the 'modal model'. According to the modal model, there are three primary types or modes of memory: the sensory register; short-term (aka working) memory; and long-term memory.

The sensory register

This is a kind of mental clearing house that holds information when it first arrives in the brain: it is the mental equivalent of flash memory in a computer.

- Each sensory mode has its own sensory register, and the different types have different storage properties, but all of them store information for only brief periods.

- The visual register, for instance, stores images – known in the jargon of cognitive science as 'icons' – for less than half a second. Items of information stored in the auditory register are called 'echoes'.

- The sensory register acts like a buffer, allowing only temporary, pre-conscious storage of a huge amount of data – most of which is irrelevant or distracting – so that your conscious mind does not suffer from sensory overload, even while the first stages of mental processing are underway.

- Information in the sensory register undergoes initial identification and analysis, for instance with processes such as 'pattern recognition', where the brain matches the sensory information to known patterns stored in the memory.

- From the mass of information momentarily held in the sensory register, only a tiny fraction makes it to the next stage of memory: short-term memory. The 'raw' data is filtered by the mechanism of attention (see page 36).

Short-term memory (STM)

This is where you hold information that you need to use in the here and now. It is sometimes described as a sort of 'mental workspace' and this practical aspect is reflected in its alternative name, 'working memory'. A classic example of STM in action is when someone tells you a phone number that you need to use. The sequence of numbers is held in your memory just long enough for you to use it. Information stored in the STM has a limited lifespan; unless it is rehearsed by repeating the information to yourself or going over it in your mind it will fade away, or decay, within a few seconds. The other process that causes loss of STM information is interference, which is where new pieces of information 'push out' older ones.

Experiments on how much people can remember over

short periods of time show that they can store more if the information comes in different formats (e.g. lists of words together with series of images, rather than simply two lists of words), and this suggests that there are actually several different types or sub-systems of STM.

- The most important ones seem to be an STM for visual imagery and one for verbal or audio information.

- The first is sometimes known as the visuo-spatial sketchpad. This is similar to a mental wipe-clean whiteboard. Images or mental maps are stored here so that the information is available for use in other mental functions, such as forward planning.

- The best understood sub-system of STM is the phonological loop, which stores 'phonemes', or units of auditory information. Usually this means the syllables that make up speech, but it also includes numbers or simply noises.

- The phonological loop itself has two components. One is a phonological store, where about two seconds worth of information is held; the other is a rehearsal device, where you repeat the information in the store over and over in a loop, but sub-vocally, without actually saying the words/noises. This constantly refreshes the information held in the store so that it remains accurate, which is important for the proper functioning of language abilities, such as associating sounds with meanings and learning new words.

- In addition to the visuo-spatial sketchpad and the phonological loop, evidence suggests that there may also be distinct STM sub-systems for meaning, odours and, in deaf people, sign language.

Encoding

For information to transition from the short- to long-term memory, it must be encoded. Encoding determines whether a memory will be stored for the long-term or will simply fade away and be lost forever; how long and securely it will be stored; in what form it will be stored and recalled; and how easy it will be to recall at a later date. In other words, what determines whether a STM will become a LTM?

Two key processes are 'attention' and 'rehearsal'. STM items that are significant or noticeable in some way – information that is interesting, important or emotionally charged in a positive *or* negative way – will catch and hold your attention. To hold such information your STM starts the process of rehearsal, where the temporary information cache is refreshed constantly to stop the information fading away. If you keep this up for long enough, the process of transferral to longer-term storage gets underway.

In order to become part of the brain's LTM store, a memory must be encoded, i.e. recorded as a set of memory elements that can later be reassembled to recover the memory. But…

- Encoding is not simply a one-step process, there are differing levels of encoding corresponding to different levels of storage.

- The initial encoding of a memory shifts it to a kind of intermediate memory store, where it may last for anywhere from an hour to a few days. If the information is revisited in some way – by being used, or brought to mind, or if the original stimulus that caused the memory is revisited – further encoding may lead to longer lasting storage.

- Not all encoding is equally effective, however. It involves making connections between the elements of the memory and other memories or memory elements already present in the brain. If few such connections are made, the encoding is said to be shallow.

- Deep encoding, by contrast, is where you form many strong connections between the new memory and existing ones. So, for instance, you are more likely to remember your day at the beach if it reminds you

The magic number

One of the foundational research papers of cognitive psychology was by the Harvard psychologist George Miller (1920–2012). His 1956 paper 'The Magical Number 7 Plus or Minus 2' demonstrated that the average capacity of STM – the number of bits or chunks of information it can hold – is 7 +/- 2 because of the variation between individuals; some people can remember up to nine items of information in the short term, others only five. This means that when given lists of numbers, names, letters, etc., to look at and then recite back, most people can recite a list of seven items before some of the items in the list are forgotten. The number of digits you can remember in this way is known as your 'digit-span'. This magic number does not only apply to numbers; it covers any information that can be broken into discrete packets or chunks of information, including words, concepts, images, noises or musical notes.

Miller's research prompted telephone companies to ensure that telephone numbers would not be more than seven digits long, excluding regional prefix codes. Even today most mobile numbers consist of a common prefix number followed by six digits.

of childhood holidays, or a particularly romantic day (which then ties it in with a whole host of other associations to do with love, relationships, etc.).

• You are also more likely, for instance, to remember a mathematical equation if you understand how it was derived. In these cases, the memory has been deeply encoded either because of powerful associations or because a thorough understanding involves drawing connections. Deeply encoded memories are more securely stored and easier to recall.

Long-term memory (LTM)

There are two main types of LTM: 'declarative' and 'procedural' memories, also called 'explicit' and 'implicit' memories, respectively. The declarative or explicit memories are things you know that you know (e.g. peoples' names, where you went on holiday, how much a loaf of bread costs, where your keys are). It is sometimes described as 'knowing that'. This category of memory further breaks down into 'semantic' and 'episodic' memory.

• Semantic memory involves facts and figures, names and words, and the ability to recognize objects and animals – memory linked to meaning. It is essential because it allows us to make sense of the world and to understand language.

- Episodic memory includes things that have happened, such as events, scenarios, situations, etc. This category includes autobiographical memory – memories of things that have happened to you – and is essential for your sense of identity.

Procedural or implicit memory is memory for skills, abilities or procedures; things you do without really remembering how (e.g. walking, riding a bicycle and brushing your teeth). It is sometimes described as 'knowing how'. Procedural memory seems to be a separate system from declarative memory since amnesiacs who lose the latter often retain the former. Anterograde amnesiacs – people who lose the ability to form new declarative memories – can still learn new skills, even if they can't recall having done so.

Memories as constructions

Memories are not simply little computer routines, which can be run again and again, producing the exact same response each time. Nor are they like photographic negatives, which can be repeatedly exposed to produce the exact same image. A memory is a mental experience in the present that is constructed from elements that refer to the past. For instance, your memory of eating an ice cream is constructed from mental representations of sweetness, coldness, etc. In other words, a memory is a reconstruction of the original experience. And remembering an experience is a bit like having a virtual experience that has been constructed to seem like the original. This explains why memory can be unreliable, and how different people can remember the same thing differently. It is even possible for people to remember things that never happened due to a phenomenon known as misattribution. A common example is when we remember something seen on TV, thinking it actually happened to us.

Forgetting

Forgetting can refer to failures at any stage of the memory process outlined above, ranging from decay or interference of STM to failure to encode STMs into LTMs. It can also involve failure to retrieve or recall a memory, even though that memory might still be stored. A simple example is where people are asked to remember examples of categories, and then have to write down the examples. Presented with a blank sheet of paper they may miss some out, but given a list of category headings they are then prompted to recall what they had previously appeared to forget. A more extreme example is when someone has fever delirium and starts speaking fluently in a foreign language they have not used since childhood. Such examples raise the question whether anything is truly forgotten.

Another theory of forgetting is the Freudian approach, which sees it as a 'motivated' process, i.e. a process of repression where the subconscious deliberately represses memories for various reasons. But whether forgetting is due to actual loss of memory traces or simply failure to retrieve, it is generally assumed to have an evolutionary or adaptive benefit as a mechanism that selects important and/or useful memories and prevents them from being obscured by a mass of less important ones.

LANGUAGE AND THOUGHT

The Ancient Greek historian Herodotus (*c.* 485–*c.* 425 BC) was one of the first to record a tale of the Egyptian pharaoh Psammetichus (ruled 664–610 BC) exploring the origins of language; in an experiment, children raised from birth were not spoken to and thus had no experience of language. The same tale was later told of the Mogul emperor Akbar the Great (1542–1605), Holy Roman Emperor Frederick II (1194–1250) and King James IV of Scotland (1566–1625).

These rulers were said to have been seeking the identity of the basic or primordial language, working on the assumption that some form of language must be hardwired into the human brain. The Scottish children, confined to an island with only a mute shepherd and his flock for company, were said to have spoken Hebrew, although the Scottish writer Sir Walter Scott (1771–1832) observed sceptically that 'It is more likely they would scream like their dumb nurse, or bleat like the goats and sheep on the island.' Natural experiments of this type, involving feral children brought up without language through neglect, appear to confirm Scott's intuition, showing that no language spontaneously emerges.

Thinking without words

Some schools of psychology have argued that thinking is dependent on or determined by language – a position known as linguistic determinism. One proponent of this view was the behaviourist John B. Watson who argued that all thinking is actually speaking of an inaudible kind produced by 'subvocalization' (undetectable vibrations of the vocal chords). This theory, known as 'peripheralism', holds that without being able to talk it is impossible to think.

The most influential form of linguistic determinism has been the Sapir–Whorf linguistic relativity hypothesis, named after two linguists and anthropologists who argued that the differing vocabularies of different cultures affected their cognitions at the most basic level. For instance, Benjamin Lee Whorf (1897–1941) famously claimed that the Inuit, with over twenty different words for snow (or fifty if you believe the *Washington Post*), are able to perceive snow in ways that standard European language speakers are not. Much of the evidence adduced by Edward Sapir (1884–1939) and Whorf is now undermined by the fact that it is not that difficult to translate between languages such as Inuit and English.

Evidence from cross-cultural research into colour words and colour perception tends to undermine the case for linguistic determinism. Although many cultures and languages recognize fewer basic colour terms than English, testing shows that people in those cultures can recognize all the same colours as those with more colour terms. In other words, cognition – in this case colour perception – does *not* depend on language.

ARTIFICIAL INTELLIGENCE (AI)

One of the most important offshoots of cognitive psychology is in AI, also known as 'machine intelligence'. This concept proposes that a machine of some sort (probably a computer) can be intelligent, although it is unclear whether this means human intelligence or some other type or degree – and indeed, how do you define human intelligence?

How could we know if a machine possessed some degree of intelligence? The prospect of AI is underpinned by the philosophy of 'functionalism', which asserts that the brain is nothing more than a machine, and that mind and consciousness are functional states of that machine. The clear analogy is with computing where functionalism sees the brain as hardware and the mind as software. An important principle of computing is that software, such as a computer programme, is multiply realizable, which means that it can be realized (run or executed) on more than one type of hardware. So, if human intelligence is a kind of software that is normally realized on the brain, perhaps it could also be realized on a different type of hardware, such as a computer. This is the contention of the theory of AI known as 'strong AI', which claims that a machine could have human-like intelligence and consciousness. By contrast, 'weak AI' claims that machines such as computers can be used to model and test human intelligence, but not that machines can actually think like humans.

Turing test vs Chinese room

Many of the fundamental questions in AI remain unresolved, in particular those relating to philosophical issues such as the nature of mind and consciousness. Two opposing points of view about the possibility of strong AI are represented by two thought experiments: the imitation game of Alan Turing (1912–54) and the Chinese room described by John Searle (b. 1932).

Turing was a British mathematician and computer science pioneer, who laid much of the groundwork for the theory and practice of electronic computers. He argued that it was meaningless to ask whether or not a machine could be intelligent, proposing instead a kind of behaviourist approach that looked at whether a computer's behaviour could *appear* intelligent. He argued that if a computer could successfully imitate a human, to the point where a person swapping text messages with the computer was unable to tell it from a real human, we would have to attribute to the computer similar faculties to a human.

But even if a computer could pass the so-called Turing test, is this the same as being intelligent? The American philosopher Searle argued not, proposing a thought experiment known as the Chinese room. Searle imagined a man in a sealed room who is fed slips of paper on which are written Chinese characters. The man does not understand Chinese, but by following a series of instructions given in a manual he can put together a response in Chinese and pass it out via a slot. To a Chinese person outside the room, the man inside the room appears to understand Chinese, even though this is not the case. Searle argues that AI is like the man in the Chinese room, able to assemble convincing responses without understanding them.

In technical terms, the AI lacks 'symbol grounding'. The wider implication of the Chinese room argument is that a machine can never be conscious in the same way as a human, since it could never understand meanings or have intentions.

3

What you need to know about

PERSONALITY AND INTELLIGENCE

What makes up an individual psyche? The study of personality and intelligence is known as 'differential' psychology because it looks at how these traits and characteristics differ between individuals. Is personality a relatively stable and consistent set of traits, independent of changing circumstance? Or is behaviour contingent upon circumstance, so that personality depends on changing situations and is mutable and inconsistent? The conflict between these two positions is known as the 'trait versus situation debate' or the 'consistency controversy'. Mainstream differential psychology generally operates on the assumption of stable core traits.

PHRENOLOGY

One of the first attempts at a scientific study of the mind and the attributes of individuals was a practice now widely dismissed as laughable pseudoscience: phrenology. Meaning the 'study of the mind', from similar roots to 'psychology', phrenology is the art and science of measuring and developing mental attributes, by means of examining the external structure of the skull.

The central tenet is that 'the brain is the organ of the mind' and its roots lie in the work of Franz Joseph Gall (1758–1828), the Viennese physician and expert on cranial anatomy. He was intrigued by an anecdotal association between bulging eyes and memory prowess, and went on to characterize other associations between mental faculties and physiognomy, or more particularly the shape of the skull. This lead to his organology theory, or the physiology of the brain. Among the revolutionary aspects of this theory was the assertion that the brain is the seat of the mind, and that mental attributes, such as personality, are determined by the structure of the brain.

Up to this point phrenology is in precise concurrence with modern psychology, which it prefigured and helped to create. Like modern psychology ...

- Phrenology also asserts that mental functions are localized in the brain, which is to say that different parts of the brain correspond to different faculties.

- But where phrenology differs is in its assertion that the size and development of these different brain organs directly affects the shape of the skull, so that an expert might determine the former by measuring the latter.

- In other words, by feeling the bumps on a person's skull, it should be possible to 'read' their personality and mental abilities.

- Phrenologists developed a list of dozens of faculties or traits that could be read from the skull, ranging from 'larceny' and the 'impulse to propagation' to 'tenderness to progeny' and 'religious sentiment'.

- It was even claimed that such traits could be cultivated or restrained by means of various exercises, an interesting undertaking in the light of ongoing debates about the power of nurture to override nature.

While its fallacies were eventually exploded, phrenology has done much to establish as legitimate the study of mind and brain, and the categorization and measurement of personality traits.

THE DIMENSIONS OF PERSONALITY

The main thrust of differential psychology is the identification and measurement of personality traits or dimensions. This is sometimes known as the psychometric approach, a field of endeavour founded by the eccentric Victorian scientist Francis Galton (1822–1911). Psychometrics usually involves statistical analysis of tests for different traits, to allow identification of underlying principles or dimensions.

Psychometrics and the Big Five

In 1936 the American psychologist Gordon W. Allport (1897–1967), one of the founders of the psychology of personality, identified over 18,000 terms describing personal characteristics, and even when he trimmed this to words describing core traits he was left with nearly 5,000. Allport distinguished between common traits, which everyone has more or less, and individual, particular traits. Although Allport argued against a psychology that restricted itself to the common traits (known as the nomothetic approach), later differential psychologists focused precisely on these.

By administering batteries of tests to individuals and applying statistical analysis to their scores, it is possible to show that tests or questions that appear to pertain to different qualities or factors are actually looking at related or identical factors. So, for example:

- Conservatism, curiosity and creativity may appear to be different traits, but people tend to score on tests of these factors in similar ways, with someone who scores high on conservatism generally scoring low on curiosity.

- Scores when testing these factors for an individual will correlate to one another, while across a group these scores will tend to vary. This suggests that apparently independent traits are often actually different facets of the same thing, so that a single factor underlies diverse traits.

- Statistical analysis of tests of many different traits can reveal a much smaller number of underlying, fundamental factors.

- And because scores in tests of this trait fall along a spectrum, these factors are often called 'dimensions'.

- Traits such as conservatism, curiosity and creativity, along with others such as sophistication, and analytical and artistic tendencies are associated with an underlying factor that differential psychologists call 'openness'.

There is a consensus in psychology around what are known as the Big Five personality dimensions: extraversion; agree-ableness; conscientiousness; neuroticism or emotional

Francis Galton – the inveterate measurer

Galton, a relative of Charles Darwin (1809–82) and an eminent scientist and explorer, had an obsessive fascination with measuring and, though this could often be useful, it could also be highly suspect. One example was his system for rating the attractiveness of women across Britain so that he could draw up a map, or his European atlas of moral reliability, which also showed Britain as the most trustworthy place, and the Greeks and Turks as the worst liars.

On reading Darwin's theories of evolution, Galton was particularly struck by the concept of selective breeding, and he applied these principles to enhancing the stock of the human race through a new science he called 'eugenics'. Galton launched a programme of testing, using a booth where people could come and undertake a battery of tests, including pioneering tests of intelligence and other aspects of psychology. Galton also pioneered the statistical analysis of biometric data, coining terms such as 'correlation' to describe relationships that he uncovered in the data.

stability; and openness. Whether or not intelligence should be included alongside these as a personality trait is debatable, but it too is a dimension or spectrum (see page 61). According to some analyses, intelligence varies with or correlates to openness.

Poles of the Big Five dimensions

Extraversion	Introversion
Talkative, sociable, gregarious, brash, boastful, arrogant, assertive, confident, poised, adventurous, enthusiastic, lively, cheerful, demonstrative, dramatic, loud, boorish	Shy, retiring, reclusive, quiet, introspective, thoughtful, cautious, modest, gloomy, meek, loner, reserved, stand-offish, listless, timid, unpretentious, reticent, diffident
Conscientiousness	**Irresponsibility**
Dependable, neat, uptight, hard-working, responsible, orderly, anal, steadfast, tidy, scrupulous, persevering, stubborn, organized, ethical, dutiful, strait-laced, plodding	Breezy, easy-going, relaxed, disorganized, capricious, self-indulgent, fickle, careless, untidy, unscrupulous, quitter, impatient
Openness	**Close-mindedness**
Original, deep and complex thinker, creative, imaginative, liberal, rebellious, artistic, nonconforming, tolerant of ambiguity, independent, questioning, unpredictable	Conservative, traditional, likes things clear cut, old-fashioned, small-minded, conformist, unimaginative, predictable, conventional, doesn't like change, straight, square
Agreeable	**Disagreeable**
Good-natured, cooperative, trusting, altruistic, helpful, kind, tender-minded, compassionate, gentle, sympathetic, compliant	Irritable, assertive, headstrong, critical, antagonistic, hostile, suspicious, selfish, hard, jealous, stubborn, wary, cynical, surly, tough-minded, cold, argumentative
Neuroticism	**Emotional stability**
Anxious, insecure, depressed, worrier, self-conscious, tense, guilty, negative, whiny, self-doubting, low self-esteem, self-pitying, temperamental, thin-skinned, vulnerable	Balanced, self-confident, self-assured, thick-skinned, calm, objective, even-tempered, measured, controlled, cool, collected, serene

Extraversion–introversion

Although dominant, the Big Five model is not the only way of categorizing or grouping personality traits. Other influential models have included the Sixteen Personality Factor Questionnaire from British-American psychologist Raymond Cattell (1905–98) and the Type theory of Anglo-German psychologist Hans Eysenck (1916–97), who in his lifetime was the most cited psychologist in the world. Eysenck argued that agreeableness and conscientiousness are actually aspects of a single, underlying personality dimension, which he called 'psychoticism', and which made up part of a three-factor model with dimensions of neuroticism-stability and extraversion-introversion.

Eysenck did much to popularize the concept of extraversion-introversion, although the terms themselves were coined by the Swiss psychoanalyst Carl Gustav Jung (1875–1961) in his 1921 book *Psychological Types*. Eysenck analyzed personality data from 700 ex-servicemen he was treating, concluding that variance in their scores could mostly be traced back to a single underlying factor. Adapting Jung's terminology of extraversion and introversion, Eysenck labelled this factor 'E'.

- Such a powerful determinant of psychology, he believed, must have a basis in biology – in other words, it must be hardwired into the brain.

- Eysenck believed that a person's 'E' rating or score depends on their level of cortical arousal or excitability – the intensity of their brain activity and the speed at which they process information.

- Introverts have higher levels of cortical arousal and so are more sensitive to external stimulus, which can overload their information-processing abilities, and accordingly they act to limit exposure to stimulus by minimizing social contact and excitement.

- Extraverts, by contrast, have lower levels of cortical arousal and hence seek to compensate for this by seeking higher levels of external stimulation.

- However, the British psychologist Jeffrey Gray (1934–2004) overturned this idea in 1970 with his Reinforcement Sensitivity theory. He argued that extraverts have more sensitive neurological reward systems, so that they are more motivated to seek social interactions because they derive more benefit in terms of pleasurable neurochemical stimulation.

Eating, bleeding and the 'humours'

For most of the ancient and medieval periods, the dominant paradigm for understanding personality and human psychology was the 'humoral theory' developed by the ancient Greeks. Bodily fluids – or 'humours' – were linked to an all-encompassing system of the qualities and elements that make up the world. So, the four elements (earth, air, fire and water) and the four qualities (wet, dry, cold and hot) correspond to the four humours: black bile (cold and dry), phlegm (cold and moist), yellow bile (hot and dry) and blood (hot and moist).

The humoral system passed down through Islamic scholars to the medieval and early modern world, along with the correlation of the humours to the four basic temperaments: melancholic, phlegmatic, choleric and sanguine. It was believed that an excess of any one humour will produce the associated temperament so that, for instance, an excess of yellow bile will result in a choleric (fiery and quick to anger) temperament. In Shakespeare's *Hamlet*, for instance, the root of Ophelia's melancholy is understood to be drying of the brain. Psychological treatment was effected by regulating the relevant humour, for instance by bleeding to drain it or consuming food or medicine to counteract its qualities (e.g. eating cold, wet foods to counteract the hot, dry yellow bile).

PSYCHODYNAMIC PERSONALITY THEORIES

A very different strand of personality psychology emerged from the psychodynamic movement, which started under Freud and was diversified by others such as Alfred Adler (1870–1937) and Jung. Freud had initially developed concepts of the topography of the psyche, dividing mental space into regions such as the unconscious, preconscious and conscious. In 1920 he outlined his influential 'structural' model of human personality, which he believed had a three-part structure, comprising the ego, the superego and the id (from the Latin terms for the 'I', the 'super-I' and the 'it').

Monsters of the id

Freud described the id as the part of the mind that includes hardwired, 'animal' instincts, such as the sex drive or libido, which he viewed as one of the primary sources of psychic energy that motivates the personality. The id seeks pleasure through instant gratification and experiences pain when this is thwarted. It takes no account of the external world.

A newborn is wholly id, but conflict with the realities of the external world causes the maturing child to develop the ego, the executive module that tries to meet the demands of the id by negotiating the real world. The ego is rational but purely practical; morality and ethics from the family and wider society feed into the formation of the superego, which monitors the ego and the id and suppresses or rewards thoughts and behaviours with guilt or pride. Freud saw an adult personality as being like an iceberg: the ego and superego are above the surface of consciousness, but the vast bulk of the id lurks beneath in the unconscious.

Adler and Jung

Freud had a series of acolytes who would be anointed as heirs apparent to the stewardship of the movement he had created known as 'psychoanalysis' – or the 'psychodynamic movement' because it concerned the dynamics of the psyche – only to undergo dramatic breaks with him when they deviated from his dogma.

The Austrian physician Alfred Adler came to reject Freud's insistence on sex as the primary engine of human personality, believing instead that power and power relations are the drivers of personality, developing concepts such as sibling rivalry, the importance of birth order in determining personality, and the inferiority complex. Adler argued that a child's attempts to compensate for or avoid feelings of inferiority direct the development of personality. Meanwhile, in adults who have failed to cope with feelings of inferiority, a maladaptive system of unconscious desires, thoughts and feelings is created, warping the workings of the conscious mind: what psychoanalysts called a 'complex'.

Jung was another acolyte who suffered a grievous break with his mentor and rejected Freud's emphasis on sex, instead viewing the libido as a more generalized source of psychic energy and the personality as more than simply a prisoner of the past. Jung believed that:

- The ultimate aspiration of the psyche was 'individuation', a process of self-acceptance and successful integration of the parts of the personality into a harmonious whole.

- He also emphasized the role in human personality of unconscious forces, or phenomena, which he called 'archetypes' and which he said are part of a collective, shared unconscious, beyond the personal unconscious of the individual.

- These archetypes, which are perhaps hardwired into the human brain, help to animate and organize thoughts, feelings and desires. The archetypes include aspects of personality, such as the Persona (roles or masks that people adopt in response to different situations or cues), the Shadow (the dark antithesis of the Persona), and the Animus and Anima (male and female aspects contained within everyone's psyche).

DEFINING INTELLIGENCE

Psychologists struggle to agree on a definition of intelligence, but the business of measuring it has nonetheless become one of the central concerns of differential psychology. The dominant view of intelligence is that it represents the individual's ability to adapt to the environment. A good summary comes from the American Psychological Association's 1996 Task Force on intelligence: '[the] ability to understand complex ideas, to adapt effectively to the environment, to learn from experience, to engage in various forms of reasoning, to overcome obstacles by taking thought.' But the importance of intelligence testing has lent weight to operational definitions of intelligence, which means defining intelligence in terms of the tests themselves, hence the observation of psychologist Edwin Boring (1886–1968) that 'intelligence is what intelligence tests measure'.

What IQ is and isn't

The most familiar measure of intelligence is IQ, which stands for intelligence quotient. A quotient is a ratio of two values. Originally devised to measure children's intelligence, IQ was defined as the ratio of the child's mental age to their chronological age, multiplied by 100. Thus, if a child's mental age were exactly the same as their chronological age, their ratio would be 1 and their IQ would be precisely 100. This will not work for adults because intellectual development generally stops at around the age of eighteen, whereas chronological age does not.

Today an IQ is defined as the ratio of an individual's score to the average score of a whole population of people of comparable age, so that someone who scores 100 sits at the centre of the normal distribution of potential scores and is of average intelligence. The nature of the reference population depends on the IQ test itself; the two most popular are the Stanford–Binet and the Wechsler. Someone with a score of 110 on the Wechsler scale would be in the 75th percentile, which means they scored higher than 75 percent of the population. Only one person in a hundred would be expected to get an IQ score of 135 on the Wechsler scale.

So what is an IQ test?

- It generally consists of a range of questions that challenge abilities such as verbal reasoning, vocabulary, mental arithmetic, logic, visual reasoning, mental rotation (rotating images in your mind's eye) and others.

- A properly validated IQ test has been tested on thousands of people, whose scores are used to calibrate the scale against which results are measured.

- IQ tests give only a snapshot of performance at a certain time, and it is instructive to consider what IQ tests do not measure. For instance, IQ tests do not measure knowledge, wisdom, creativity or memory, although they can all be shown to be closely related to IQ. Memory power, especially short-term memory, is a particularly important component of intelligence.

- Also, IQ tests do not measure valuable personal qualities or traits such as compassion, resilience, discipline or fairness, nor do they test emotional skills, sometimes described as emotional intelligence.

General intelligence and raw, mental power

Some psychologists argue that IQ and intelligence are almost exactly the same thing. Others argue that because intelligence is not a single quality or attribute it cannot be measured by a single score. One way of approaching the subject is through a statistical analysis of tests of apparently different abilities, to examine whether they are actually aspects of a single underlying dimension, as with the Big Five personality traits (see page 60).

Statistical analysis of people's scores across all the different types of intelligence test seems to show that there is a common factor: that someone who is good at a verbal test is more likely to also be good at a mathematical test. This common factor has been called 'g', for 'general intelligence'; it is a measure of someone's raw, mental power. A useful analogy is with racing cars:

- Different cars might have different handling abilities, wheel and tyre types, etc., meaning that some cars do better in rallies on dirt tracks while others perform better on a racing circuit.

- The different handling characteristics are like a person's abilities with different types of problem (e.g. verbal v logic).

- But one factor that will boost the performance of all the cars, whatever their differences, is a more powerful engine and 'g' is the equivalent of engine power. Just as a race car with a more powerful engine is likely to win more races, whatever the course and conditions, so a person with a higher level of 'g' is more likely to score well across all types of intelligence test.

The Flynn Effect

This phenomenon was uncovered by James Flynn (b. 1934), a political scientist at the University of Otago in New Zealand. In 1984 Flynn published the first of a series of papers drawing attention to a strange trend that had previously gone unremarked: the companies that made and sold IQ tests were having to continually revise their scoring systems to maintain an average IQ of 100 because people seemed to be scoring better in IQ tests each year. Flynn discovered that in order to get the same IQ today as someone who did the same test twenty years earlier, you would have to perform much better. Or, put another way, if you got the exact same score on the exact same test, but twenty years apart, this would translate into a significantly lower IQ score in the modern day.

The reason for this continual revision of the scoring system was that the average performance seemed to be getting better year on year. Flynn discovered that, on average, people in the developed world were gaining about 0.5 IQ points a year, or about 15 IQ points over thirty years. If you went back to 1945 and used today's scoring standards, which are based on today's average performances, you would find that the average IQ was around 70, which is borderline learning disabled.

Since we have not seen a radical boost in the number of geniuses or in general intellectual attainment – while many people argue that educational standards have fallen and that attainment is lower than in the past – one suggested explanation for this is that improved diet and healthcare have led to better brains. Another is that people have become increasingly familiar with IQ-type questions through TV, computer games, newspaper puzzles, school tests, etc. A third is that Flynn has simply got his sums wrong. The evidence doesn't clearly support any of these explanations, so the Flynn effect remains a mystery.

Pinpointing the 'g' in the brain

Since there is little agreement about exactly what constitutes intelligence, it's hard to say where in the brain it is located. If we think about intelligence as a constellation of different mental functions and abilities then we can say that it is distributed all over the brain, but primarily in the cortex, the wrinkled outer layer of the brain. More specific abilities can be more precisely located – for instance, the most abstract mental functions, such as logical reasoning and forward planning, are primarily localized to the prefrontal cortex. The location of 'g', if it exists at all, is an intriguing mystery. It is unlikely, however, to simply be a property of one part of the brain and is more likely to relate to a general feature such as the speed of transmission of nervous impulses along your neurons, or an innate tendency of your neurons to make connections more or less easily.

Predictions and IQ

To reiterate, IQ is not the same as intelligence, and it fails to capture many other qualities that are important for success and talent. For any individual, a high IQ might count for less than, say, commitment and discipline; a lazy high-IQ individual, for instance, may be less likely to succeed than a diligent, hard-working low-IQ individual. But at group and population scales, IQ proves to be a remarkably powerful predictor of achievements in a host of fields, from academic success to earning power to health and happiness. We also know that:

- On average, people with a higher IQ get better grades, are more likely to be employed, earn more, get promoted more, live longer and stay healthier than those with a lower IQ score.

- Studies on the use of IQ-style testing as a tool for selecting job applicants show that its predictive power for the success of applicants is as good as exhaustive interviews, and better than other measures such as years of job experience.

- Compared to people with an IQ in the 75–90 range, those with an IQ over 110 are 88 times less likely to drop out of school, five times less likely to live in poverty and seven times less likely to end up in jail.

IQ and race

Perhaps the most contentious topic in all of psychology is the question of racial differences in IQ. A robust finding (meaning they are resistant to errors) in IQ studies is that different ethnic groups score differently, on average, in IQ tests. In America, where most of the research has been done,

African-Americans tend to score lower, on average, than whites, who in turn score lower that East Asians. Though one explanation could be that IQ tests are culturally specific and thus biased, there is a lot of evidence that the findings persist with culturally neutral tests. Another explanation is that the findings reflect socio-economic challenges and inequality but, again, analysis to control these factors suggests the findings are robust.

Now to the controversy:

- One reason for it is the fear that those with specific political and/or racial agendas will use such findings to argue that, for instance, state intervention such as funding early education boosting is likely to be ineffective on the basis that low attainment is genetically, not environmentally, determined.

- But genetic determinism faces many counterarguments. For instance, the meaning and validity of racial categorization, especially in genetic terms, is highly dubious because of the extensive racial mixing of global, and particularly American, populations, and because scientists struggle to distinguish between races at a genetic level.

- Furthermore, the race and IQ debate tends to obscure the fact that any differences, genuine or not, are small compared to individual variation. And variation between individuals is far greater than the supposed inter-group variation.

Types of intelligence

IQ tests challenge different abilities or modes of thinking, but some psychologists go further and question the coherence of intelligence as a unitary concept. It may be that intelligence is an invalid umbrella term for diverse and separate abilities or functions. The leading proponent of this 'multiple intelligences' school of thought is the American developmental psychologist Howard Gardner (b. 1943), who distinguishes between eight different types of intelligence, which fall into four different classes. He claims there are:

- Two types of 'thinking' intelligence: verbal-linguistic and logical-mathematical.

- Three types of 'sensational' (i.e. involving the senses) intelligence: visuo-spatial, body-kinaesthetic and auditory-musical.

- Two types of 'communicational' intelligence: intrapersonal and interpersonal.

- And a 'naturalist' intelligence.

Social and emotional intelligence

The American psychologist E.L. Thorndike (1874–1949) coined the term 'social intelligence' as far back as 1920. He defined it as the ability to understand and relate to people. Later, social intelligence was used to explain the evolution of the human brain. According to some theories, humans evolved larger brains as a result of their developing social skills, creating a more complex human society and a greater need for still better social intelligence and hence larger brains.

Focus on cognitive skills equivalent to social or communication skills intensified in the 1990s, and they were rebranded as emotional intelligence (EI). EI plays an important role not just in relationships and any sphere where people interact or emotions come into play, but also in how well people can monitor, comprehend and regulate their own emotions, needs and feelings. People with high levels of EI are more likely to be self-aware, confident, balanced and fulfilled, and also to be better at dealing with other people. They make good salespeople, managers, team workers and leaders, as well as doing well in the caring professions.

4

What you need to know about
GROUP PSYCHOLOGY

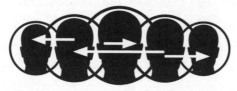

The study of how people think and behave as individuals in social situations, including how they think and behave in and as groups, is known as social psychology. This field of study received particular impetus after the Second World War, when psychologists faced up to the challenge of explaining how people could have acted as they did, especially in the light of the Holocaust. Burgeoning civil-rights consciousness and social change involving rejection of conformity and authority also led to a renewed focus on topics such as prejudice and racism.

GROUP DYNAMICS:
THE EAGLES AND RATTLERS

In 1954 eleven twelve-year olds were bussed to a remote Boy Scout camp in Robber's Cave State Park in Oklahoma. After a few days of bonding with each other the group came up with a team name: the Rattlers. They then learned that another group of eleven boys had arrived at the park the day before them and called themselves the Eagles. Researchers, led by the Turkish–American social psychologist Muzafer Sherif (1906–88), had assigned the twenty-two boys to the two groups entirely at random, but each quickly began to display a strong allegiance to their team, becoming quite aggressive when put in competition with each other for minor sporting trophies. The Eagles even burned the Rattlers' flag while the Rattlers ransacked the Eagles' cabin.

Interviewed afterwards the children characterized their own group in highly favourable terms, and the other group very unfavourably. Through the simple act of separating them, at random, into two entirely arbitrary groupings, Sherif had apparently turned twenty-two, perfectly ordinary kids into something resembling the *Lord of the Flies*. This experiment led Sherif and colleagues to develop their Realistic Conflict theory of group dynamics, in which competition for resources or other forms of conflict is at the root of prejudice and drives positive in-group attribution and ill-feeling towards outsiders.

Klee, Kandinsky and social identity

The Polish-British social psychologist Henri Tajfel (1919–82) came to believe that the Robber's Cave experiment could be explained even more simply than Sherif had envisaged. In a classic experiment in 1970, Tajfel stripped group identity down to its basics with his minimal group paradigm. He divided teenage boys into two groups labelled Klee or Kandinsky. Though supposedly based on the boys' preferences when shown pictures of artworks by abstract expressionist painters Paul Klee and Wassily Kandinsky, the assignations were in fact entirely random. The boys then worked individually through a task in which they had to allocate very small monetary rewards to fellow group members (in-group) or members of the other group (out-group).

Tajfel found that the boys favoured the distribution that maximized the difference between in- and out-group rewards, even when that meant the in-group getting less overall. This was despite the boys having had no contact with and knowing nothing about their group or its members, and it persisted even when the boys were told the group assignments were random.

Findings such as these led Tajfel to develop a social identity theory, which describes how the simple fact of group membership triggers a set of attitudes and drives a series of consequences.

- Being part of the in-group drives individuals to look for ways to differentiate themselves from the out-group, and to enhance their self-image by discriminating against the out-group.

- Social categorization – dividing the world into us and them, and becoming aware of group boundaries – leads to social identification, adopting the identity of the group to which one has become assigned, which in turn leads to...

- Social comparison, when people seek to enhance in-group self-esteem through unfavourable comparisons to the out-group.

Social identity theory says that prejudice is an inevitable consequence of social categorization, and that the only resource that needs to be scarce to drive conflict and prejudice is self-esteem.

Social cognition, attribution and bias

But what is the mechanism underlying social identity theory? Why should humans be so prone to social categorization? One answer is in the way we make attributions in a social context, and the evolutionary rationale that shapes this 'social cognition'.

An early theory about social cognition assumed that people made choices based on logic and calculations, as a computer might. Yet people do not think like this; we make rapid, messy choices using logic that is fuzzy at best. In place of the social computer model, a better fit might be the 'cognitive miser' hypothesis. This says that we seek to minimize the expenditure of cognitive resources by using the minimum necessary information and processing power, and by adopting shortcuts and rules-of-thumb to maximize the efficiency of cognitive processing. Such strategies are known as 'heuristics', and their use can be inferred from some intriguing findings in social psychology.

The 'central trait' and how to influence people

In 1946 the Polish-American psychologist Solomon Asch (1907–96) asked people to read a biography describing a fictional person with a few adjectives. They were then asked to choose some further descriptions that fit the main character. But by changing a single word in the biography, altering 'warm' to 'cold', Asch found that the attributions made to the fictional person changed dramatically. If the biography included the adjective 'warm', follow-up attributions included generous, sociable and humorous; if 'cold' they called him mean, withdrawn and humourless. Asch deduced that the cold-warm personality dimension is what he called a 'central trait' – one that has a strong influence on other attributions.

Unconscious prejudices

Central traits are related to a similar phenomenon, known as the 'halo effect'. This is where positive attributions around one trait or characteristic spill over onto others, as if the person or thing has a halo that casts a beneficent glow on all their attributes. First observed in 1907, it was labelled the 'halo error' in 1920 by Edward Thorndike.

The classic example is that physically attractive people are deemed to be more intelligent, nicer, more competent, etc., simply because of their looks. The opposite of the halo effect is the horns or 'give a dog a bad name' effect, in which one negative attribution triggers others. For instance, it has been shown that the same paper will be graded more harshly by a teacher who thinks it has come from a problem student than if they believe it to have been written by a model student. Versions of the halo and horn effects can be seen at work in prejudices such as racism and sexism, where, for instance, masculinity is associated with positive traits such as control, competence and rationality, while femininity may be associated with emotionality, weakness and timidity, etc. Even names and faces can trigger automatic judgements and assumptions.

THE NEED TO CONFORM

Muzafer Sherif, of Robber's Cave fame (see page 82), won his doctorate with an elegant study in the 1920s, showing the power of group membership and social interaction in shaping fundamental mental processes such as cognition. The study involved:

- Volunteers in a pitch-black room, where a dot of bright light was shone on the wall. Although the dot was stationary, autokinetic (involuntary, usually unnoticed) movements of the eye muscles, in the context of the lack of any frame of reference in the darkened room, meant that to the test subject the dot appeared to be moving.

- When Sherif placed three subjects in the room and asked them to speak aloud their estimates of the dot's motion, it was found that although the perceived motion was purely subjective and thus must have been different for each participant, their estimates quickly converged.

- Each group arrived at a tacitly agreed estimate of the amount of motion, without having been asked to and without discussing it.

- Tested individually a week later, participants stuck

with their group's original estimate, showing, Sherif concluded, that they had internalized the tacitly agreed norm. The power of social cognition – in this case the urge to agree with others – is powerful enough to affect perception.

Line judge

A more famous demonstration of a related effect was to come, with Solomon Asch's 1951 conformity experiment. Asch asked subjects to compare the length of a single line to three reference lines and judge which of the three was the same. The correct answer was obvious, but if tested as part of a group, the other members of which had been instructed to give the same wrong answer, he found that, on average, one-third of test subjects would agree with the majority even though they were obviously incorrect. Three-quarters of participants conformed at least once, and only one in four refused to conform.

The experiment was interpreted in the light of the recent horrors of the Second World War, and the puzzle of why so many 'ordinary' Germans had apparently supported the Nazis. An attempt to replicate the study in 1980 found that in only 1 out of 396 trials did someone conform to the incorrect judgement, suggesting that Asch's finding was a product of its more deferential and conformist era.

Following orders

Asch's was just one of a string of social psychology experiments that cast light on the challenging psychology of Nazi collaborators. More controversial research included Milgram's obedience to authority study and the Stanford prison experiment (see page 90).

In 1961 the American social psychologist Stanley Milgram (1933–84) advertized for men to take part in what was billed as a study of learning. This is what happened:

- The test subjects were divided, apparently at random, into 'learning' or 'teaching' roles, although in reality all the 'learners' were Milgram's associates.

- The 'teachers' were then shown the learners being fitted with electroshock administering gear. The teachers went into the next room and were told to operate an electric shock generator (they didn't know it was fake), with thirty switches marked from 15 volts (labelled 'slight shock') to 450 volts (labelled 'danger – severe shock').

- A lab-coat-wearing supervisor then asked the learner some questions and directed the unwitting test subject to administer shocks in response to 'wrong' answers.

- As the shocks increased in power, the teacher/test subject could hear increasingly loud (pretend) shouts and screams from the neighbouring room. If they objected to administering the shocks, the 'supervisor' simply read from a script statements such as 'the experiment requires you to continue' or 'you have no other choice but to continue'.

- Milgram found that two-thirds of the teachers would continue all the way up to the highest level.

- 'The extreme willingness of adults to go to almost any lengths on the command of an authority,' Milgram concluded, 'constitutes the chief finding of the study and the fact most urgently demanding explanation.' Today Milgram's experiment is regarded as ethically impermissible, and indeed many of the participants were profoundly upset by their experience.

The Stanford prison experiment

Philip Zimbardo (b. 1933) of Stanford University in California tweaked Milgram's obedience-to-authority experiment to show that test subjects were more likely to give worse shocks if they were given laboratory coats than if they wore their own clothes with large name tags. Suspecting the uniforms and roles might play a part in cueing or permitting compliance with authority, he devised what would become one of the most notorious experiments in psychology.

- In 1971, Zimbardo advertized for healthy young men to volunteer for a prisoner/guard role-play experiment, and participants were randomly assigned to be one or the other. 'Guards' were outfitted with beige uniforms, nightsticks and mirrored glasses, and directed simply to keep the prisoners incarcerated and not to use violence.

- 'Prisoners' went through a realistic simulation of arrest, were given prison gowns, nylon caps and ankle chains to wear, and were confined in the basement of Stanford University's psychology department. This had been mocked up to give a reasonable simulation of a prison. Both guards and prisoners were informed at the beginning that the roles had been randomly assigned and that they could leave at any time.

- The experiment was originally scheduled to last for two weeks, but in the course of just six days a remarkable transformation occurred. Both prisoners and guards came to inhabit their roles to a shocking degree. Prisoners became meek, submissive and withdrawn, seeming to forget that they were there on a voluntary basis. The guards became aggressive, controlling and increasingly sadistic. They treated the prisoners in an increasingly cruel and inhumane fashion and eventually some of the prisoners became traumatized, forcing Zimbardo to abort the trial after less than a week.

Though wildly controversial then and since, the Stanford prison experiment seemed to prove that socially or culturally created 'social scripts', mediated through institutions and roles, could profoundly influence behaviour. It appeared that, with the aid of a few simple props such as a uniform and sunglasses, anyone could be transformed into a sadist.

5

What you need to know about
GROWING UP

The study of how minds develop and learn is known as 'developmental psychology', some aspects of which cross over into philosophy, touching on age-old debates such as that between nativism and empiricism, two different philosophies of knowledge and its acquisition.

EMPIRICISM, RATIONALISM AND NATIVISM

Empiricism says that all knowledge comes from experience, and in developmental terms it leads to a concept of the infant mind as a blank slate, devoid of prior cognitive structures, which develop as the the child interacts with the world. But empiricism has been challenged since at least the time of Plato (*c.* 428–347 BC). Intriguingly, he used an example of sensory relativism to refute the claim that all knowledge must derive from experience of the world, pointing out that experience can be misleading.

If one person enters a room having been outside in a snowstorm, while another comes from stoking a furnace, they will disagree about whether the room is hot or cold. A popular modern version of this experiment teaches children how the senses work – they put one hand in a bowl of hot water and the other in a bowl of freezing water, and then immerse both hands in tepid water and try to judge the temperature of the water.

Plato advocated a position known as 'rationalism', in which reason and logic are the basis of knowledge (logic can show that some things are necessarily true, such as $2 + 2 = 4$). But he also recognized another alternative, nativism, which suggests that knowledge is innate or native to the mind. The debate between empiricism, rationalism and nativism would play out in the development of developmental psychology and its most influential theories.

A BRIEF HISTORY OF DEVELOPMENTAL PSYCHOLOGY

Perhaps the first to attempt a scientific look at the developmental psychology of the child was Charles Darwin who, in 1877, published a study based on observations of his son Doddy, and how he tried to communicate. Then in 1882 the German physiologist Wilhelm Preyer (1841–97) published his seminal book *The Mind of the Child*, marking the formal start of developmental psychology. This too was based on close observation of his own child, in this case the first two and a half years of his daughter's life.

Freudian psychosexual theory, from the oral to the phallic

Freud saw childhood as the proving ground for lifelong personality features, both normal and neurotic. He viewed the central driving force as the libido, a kind of psychic sexual energy or drive present from birth. This in turn led him to develop a psychosexual theory of development, with stages defined by the erogenous zones on which libidinous energy is focused at each phase. The key stages are:

- The oral stage: centred on the mouth and lips, when pleasure is derived from sucking liquid and putting food and other things in the mouth. Freud said that oral 'styles' prefigured later personality types so that, for instance, babies particularly fixated on putting things in their mouths – known as 'oral incorporation' – might become greedy and materialistic in later life. Those who were orally aggressive and fond of biting might in later life develop traits such as sarcasm and bitterness, characterized by terms such as 'biting' wit or 'spewing' bile.

- From around the age of one to two, the anal stage: the focus is on developing control of the bowels and bladder, and libidinous energy is derived from retaining or expelling faeces. Freud pointed to toilet training as a crucial influence on later personality. Toddlers who were harshly criticized for not controlling their bowels might become anally retentive out of fear of improper defecation. In later life this might manifest as stinginess and selfishness. Children praised for successful defecation might become anal expulsives, likely to become generous and creative.

- Between the ages of two and three, Freud said that children enter the phallic stage. The genital stage might be more accurate though, since he said that for both boys and girls the libido at this time is centred around the genitals, but in Freudian terminology the genital stage comes later, around puberty. In the phallic stage torrid psychosexual dramas play out in the child's unconscious mind, leading to phenomena such as castration anxiety, penis envy, the Oedipal conflict (where boys develop an incestuous desire for the mother and a rivalry with the father) and the formation of the superego.

- The phallic phase is followed by a period of latency, only for the libido to erupt again at puberty and trigger the genital phase. In this stage the adolescent object of affection and desire moves from parents to peers, and psychosexual urges develop from the purely narcissistic to allow sharing, altruism and loving.

Freud's emphasis on sex and the genitals scandalized his contemporaries and turned many of his own followers against him. Although their cultural impact has been immense, his theories did not have a great influence on developmental psychology because of their lack of grounding in evidence and experimental verification.

Skinner and his baby box

The importance of experiments, and of building theories on what could be observed, was the impetus behind the behaviourist school of psychology. Behaviourism was strictly empiricist, proposing that learning takes place through interactions with the environment in a process known as conditioning. Pavlov's work with dogs (see p 98) demonstrated what came to be known as classical conditioning, in which behaviour is a response elicited by a stimulus from the environment. The influential American behaviourist B.F. Skinner (1904–90) developed the concept of operant conditioning, in which behaviours are learned, or perhaps more accurately trained, through reinforcement.

Inspired by Pavlov's dictum 'control the environment and you will see order in behaviour', Skinner designed an

Pavlov's dogs

In 1904 the Russian physiologist Pavlov had won a Nobel prize for his work on the nervous control of canine digestion and salivation. In the process he had perfected surgical techniques for *in vivo* (i.e. using living entities) collection of saliva and gastric secretions in dogs, providing an experimental tool with which it might be possible to investigate and quantify behavioural responses to psychological processes. Pavlov had observed that dogs began to salivate on catching sight of the workers who brought their foods, a response he called 'psychic salivation'.

Exploring this response, Pavlov was able to show that dogs could be conditioned to transfer this salivation response from a natural stimulus (sensing food) to a neutral stimulus, such as ringing a bell. He developed a technical jargon for the process, in which the dogs went from giving an unconditioned response (UCR) to an unconditional stimulus (UCS), to giving a conditioned response (CR) to a conditional stimulus (CS). The jargon even lent itself to algebraic formulations.

apparatus for demonstrating operant conditioning in mice or rats, in a tightly controlled environment. Later known as the Skinner box, this is a light- and sound-proofed cube, usually around 30 centimetres (1 foot) on each side, containing an 'operandum' or 'manipulandum', which is a device such as a lever, bar or button that is pressed to trigger the release of a reward, e.g. food dropping into a hopper. The operandum provides positive reinforcement for whatever task or behaviour is being conditioned. Negative reinforcement could come from loud noises or electrified floors.

Skinner believed that operant conditioning through positive or negative reinforcement could essentially explain all human behaviour, including childhood development. He sought to apply his theories to his own children and famously designed an 'air crib' (or 'baby box') for his infant daughter in 1944. This was a climate-controlled crib that would provide a safe, hygienic, easy-to-clean and comfortable space for a baby, freeing it from excessive swaddling and making parents' lives easier. The crib was designed to raise the sleeping area to a more convenient height for parents, while also giving the child a better vantage point without sacrificing safety.

Skinner's daughter slept and played in the crib for the first two years of her life and about 300 commercially produced air cribs were sold. Follow-up research suggested that they were successful in providing safe and beneficial environments but they never caught on; inevitably the air crib became conflated in the public mind with the Skinner box and its connotations of confined laboratory animals undergoing impersonal conditioning trials.

Bandura's social learning

Although behaviourism fell out of favour after the Second World War, conditioning still figured heavily in accounts of learning, particularly in the social learning theory of the Canadian-American psychologist Albert Bandura (b. 1925), which acted as a kind of bridge between behaviourism and cognitive psychology, and even included elements of Freudian theory. In Bandura's model, operant conditioning is mediated by cognitive processes, specifically when children observe social models and use them to construct mental models. He said that children observe the world around them, encode behaviours they see and then try to imitate some through following mental models of them. A well-known demonstration of this was the Bobo doll experiment (see page 103). The resulting behaviours are then either positively or negatively reinforced by the feedback they get from the social context.

This model could help explain, for instance, the origins of gender-specific behaviours. According to social learning, boys and girls model their behaviour on what are signalled to them as appropriate role models, and then get positive or negative reinforcement depending on how their behaviour conforms to stereotypical gender roles. This acts to mould the child's behaviour accordingly.

Bandura looked to Freudian concepts to explain what

motivates modelling and its effect on the child. Freud discussed how the child will seek to win approbation and enhance self-esteem by identifying with a role model and internalizing the image that they admire. Bandura similarly claimed that through modelling another individual's behaviour, the child also comes to model their beliefs, attitudes and values.

Bonding and attachment

Behaviourism was often characterized as cold and inhumane because it tended to dismiss or downplay cognitions and emotions as 'mere' conditioned responses. For instance, the behaviourist rationale for children's attachment to their parents is that this is simply cupboard love – a rational response to parental provision of resources. A behaviourist explanation for babies' crying is that it acts as an unpleasant stimulus that elicits a caring response from parents in order to diminish the stimulus. An obvious flaw in this argument is that the easiest way for a parent to limit exposure to the negative stimulus would be to move away rather than engage with the infant.

Bowlby's attachment theory

An alternative, more humanistic approach grew out of the work of British psychiatrist John Bowlby (1907–90), whose work with troubled children in the 1930s and 1940s led him to forge a link between childhood neglect and later emotional difficulties. Bowlby had a nativist approach, theorizing that evolution has equipped humans with an innate tendency to form attachments. He was influenced by the work in the 1930s of Austrian ethologist Konrad Lorenz (1903–89), on imprinting in animals (see page 105).

Bowlby's arguments were as follows:

- He believed that it makes evolutionary sense for babies to seek comfort and protection, and for parents to want to provide it.

- Accordingly, animals will evolve species-specific mechanisms to promote bonding and attachment, and humans are no different. Babies instinctively display what Bowlby called 'social releasers' – for example crying – that elicit care-giving responses from adults, who are instinctively programmed to respond.

- Both child and adult are also programmed to form attachment bonds, and Bowlby argued that, at least initially, the child instinctively forms one primary attachment. He did not view this attachment as a purely transactionary phenomenon, but as a 'lasting psychological connectedness between human beings'.

- It forms the basis for the healthy, well-adapted development that follows, providing the infant with security and the confidence to explore the world and risk interactions with others.

Bobo dolls and play/aggression

Bandura demonstrated his theory of social learning through modelling with an experiment involving 'Bobo dolls' – large inflatable toys with weighted bases, painted as clowns – that could be knocked over only to spring back up again. In his study, three- to six-year-old boys and girls were playing in a room when an adult came in and started to punch and kick an adult-size Bobo doll. When the children were later given a child-size Bobo doll to play with, Bandura found that those who had observed aggressive adult 'models' were much more likely to be aggressive with the doll, and that boys were more likely to be aggressive than girls, and more likely to imitate male adult behaviour. Moreover, viewing such behaviour on videotape could also prompt aggressive responses.

Bandura concluded that the study provided strong support for his social learning theory, and it has often been cited as proof of the potential for violent imagery – as on TV or in videogames – to 'contaminate' impressionable young minds. However, the study has been criticized for misinterpreting the children's responses, since their aggressive behaviour was arguably more playful than violent and the children acted as they did because they felt they were being asked to do so.

Bowlby also believed that lack of attachment in early years (aka 'maternal deprivation') could have severe consequences in later life. Neglected or maternally deprived children will be withdrawn and developmentally challenged, and will carry maladaptive behaviour and psychology into adult life. Outcomes that Bowlby linked to maternal deprivation included delinquency, reduced intelligence, aggression and depression. Some evidence to back up his theories was provided by the maternal separation experiments with monkeys carried out by Harry Harlow (1905–81).

When monkeys are reared without mothers

Harlow was an American psychologist who, from 1959, explored issues of maternal separation and infant attachment needs in a controversial series of experiments with baby rhesus monkeys. Newborn monkeys were separated from their mothers at birth and reared in isolation in cages along with two surrogate 'mothers'. One was just a tube of bare wire, while the other was wire covered in a towelling cloth. Harlow showed that even when the wire 'mother' was equipped with a bottle dispensing milk, the infant monkeys preferred to spend their time clinging to the cloth 'mother'. When Harlow introduced a teddy-bear toy drummer into the cage to frighten them, the monkeys always ran to the cloth mother.

The experiment seemed to prove several points:

Lorenz, imprinting and attachment at first sight

Konrad Lorenz became famous for his work on the phenomenon of imprinting in geese. He discovered that when goslings hatch there is a critical window during which they form a strong attachment to whatever is in their visual field, i.e. they are genetically programmed to imprint on significant visual stimuli, which in nature would be their care-giver. Lorenz gave a striking demonstration of the phenomenon when he separated a clutch of goose eggs and let half of the hatchlings imprint on a female goose and half on him. The goslings were then mixed together under a box and Lorenz and the goose were placed opposite one another, and when the box was lifted the mass of goslings sorted itself neatly into the two original groups, one going to Lorenz and the other to the goose.

Lorenz and others found that the critical period is within twelve to seventeen hours after hatching, and that if imprinting does not take place within thirty-two hours it will not happen at all. Imprinting is believed to be a one-off, irreversible event. Lorenz had proved that, for some creatures at least, attachment is an instinctive, hardwired response.

- That mere sustenance is not the driving force behind attachment, with security and comfort privileged over food. When the privated monkeys became adults they were found to exhibit disturbed or 'delinquent' behaviour. They struggled to form relationships with other monkeys, were withdrawn and/or aggressive and did not know how to mate. When privated females did become mothers they were neglectful.

- However, critics pointed out that the delinquency of the privated monkeys could just as easily reflect their lack of maternal discipline in childhood and the absence of role models from which they could learn social behaviours.

- Intriguingly, a follow-up study also showed that the effects of deprivation – contrary to Bowlby's assertion – could be at least partially reversed. By introducing a kind of monkey 'therapist' (female monkeys younger than the privated subjects) to share a cage with them, the privated monkeys were induced to become more socialized and better adjusted.

- In 1962 Harlow compared monkeys reared with a cloth mother to those reared in total isolation, finding that the latter unfortunates engaged in profoundly disturbed behaviour such as hugging themselves and rocking, and that when later introduced to other monkeys they were fearful and aggressive, and prone to self-harming. Harlow was later criticized extensively on ethical grounds.

Attachment styles and the Strange Situation

Attachment is not a single, uniform process. According to a 1964 study, in the first three months of life babies display indiscriminate attachment to any care-giver, but from four months infants recognize primary carers and from seven months they show a clear preference for a single carer. By the ages of twelve to eighteen months the infant has a strong attachment to the care-giver and becomes very distressed at being separated – this is known as 'separation anxiety'. The eventual goal of attachment, however, is seen as facilitating detachment – the process of exploring the world and being a separate person.

A well-known 1978 study by American-Canadian developmental psychologist Mary Ainsworth (1913–99) explored different styles of attachment and their effect on detachment. In her Strange Situation paradigm, she tested twelve- to eighteen-month-olds in a series of situations: playing with the mother present; meeting a stranger and being left alone with her; and being left all alone and then reuniting with the mother. Based on her observations of how infants reacted to the various scenarios, Ainsworth characterized three attachment styles.

- Securely attached babies are happy to explore a strange room but with reference to their mother, crying when she leaves the room, unable to be comforted by a stranger and seeking contact on reunion.

- Anxious-avoidant infants are less interested in their mother, and while they may cry on being left alone can be comforted by a stranger.

- Ambivalent infants cry and seem insecure even when mother is present, becoming very distressed on separation but behaving ambivalently when she returns, seeking contact while pushing her away and refusing to be easily comforted.

Ainsworth's categorizations have been criticized for being reductive, simplistic and incomplete, and for being too judgemental, thereby pathologizing normal behaviour and implicitly blaming mothers for it (as with the 'frigid' mother attribution in autism, see page 116).

Learning to think

Neither behaviourism nor attachment theory had much to say about cognitive development. The two big names in this field were the Swiss scientist Jean Piaget (1896–1980) and the Russian psychologist Lev Vygotsky (1896–1934), who tried to give an account of how and why children learn to think and become social, and how these two processes interact.

Piaget and constructivism

Piaget had studied natural history and philosophy but was drawn to psychology and he worked with the French psychometrician Alfred Binet (1857–1911) in around 1920. While marking the tests that were the forerunner of modern IQ tests, Piaget noticed that young children consistently made the same sort of mistakes. He was fascinated by the implication that their thinking must be different from older people, and it spurred him to develop what would become an overarching theory of universal stages of cognitive development that all children pass through. His approach or philosophy is sometimes known as 'constructivism' because it treats learning as a constructive process, though he considered himself a genetic epistemologist ('epistemology' being the study of knowledge and 'genetic' implying origins, so a genetic epistemologist is one who studies the development of knowledge and learning).

Piaget studied children's approach to problem solving and interacting with the world. Typically, he would observe an individual child who had been asked to play or solve a problem, especially when they had been asked to do so in a new way. Over sixty years Piaget built up a model of intellectual development consisting of four main stages:

Now you see it, now …

Object permanence is the ability to understand that things continue to exist even when you can't see them. A child is shown a favourite toy and is delighted, but then a blanket is put over the toy. Children under around eight months old are not readily capable of looking under the blanket and may seem confused or upset or simply move on, because they seem to operate on the basis that if they cannot see it the toy must not be there. Similarly monkeys with lesions to the prefrontal cortex – a region at the front of the brain associated with higher level reasoning and planning – cannot display object permanence, suggesting that in babies under eight months the prefrontal cortex has not matured enough to develop this ability. Object permanence is different from the phenomenon underlying a child's belief that if they cannot see, they cannot be seen (see 'Theory of mind', page 112), but it may explain their delight at games of 'peekaboo' when an adult hides their face.

- Sensorimotor (zero to two years).

- Preoperational (two to seven years).

- Concrete operational (seven to twelve years).

- Formal operational (twelve years plus).

At each stage, Piaget said, children can achieve different levels of mastery, and progression is not necessarily linear. Especially in the later stages, he conceived of progression as a kind of spiral, with progress in one stage enabling reworking of earlier stages, which in turn could aid more progress.

From the egocentric to invariance

In the 'sensorimotor' stage the infant begins with only innate reflexes and develops the ability to repeat actions and explore new ones, along with cognitive achievements such as coordination, representation of external things as mental concepts, and ideas of object permanence and intentionality (understanding that the self and other people and things can have meaning and purpose).

In the 'preoperational' stage children are restricted to their own point of view (egocentrism) and can only focus on one aspect of a situation – whatever happens to grab their attention. There is no logical flow to their thought as they leap from one concept to another via simple juxtaposition, and they cannot account for their own thought.

These restrictions are slowly worked through in the 'concrete operational' stage, when children acquire the concept of invariance or conservation: the ability to understand that quantities persist through transformations and are finite − e.g. that six matches lined up next to each other are the same six when rearranged in a square, or that the volume of a liquid remains the same whether in a shallow bowl or a tall glass. Invariance is acquired in a set order: number, length and mass, area, weight, time and volume. In the formal operational stage, adolescents learn to conceptualize and manipulate mental models and hypotheses, allowing a higher order of thinking.

Theory of mind

A key cognitive ability that children are not born with is what psychologists call 'theory of mind': recognizing that other people have minds and understanding what they might be thinking. A classic concrete illustration of what this means is the game where a young child covers their eyes and thinks this makes them invisible; because they cannot see others, they believe they cannot be seen.

Theory of mind was first formulated in relation to chimpanzees in 1978. The primatologists David Premack and Guy Woodruff tested chimps by asking them to decide who to approach for food: a handler who is blindfolded or

Infantile amnesia and neurogenesis

Although some people claim to remember their early months and even being born, it is widely accepted that in fact people cannot remember anything before their first eighteen to twenty-four months, and usually not before the age of three to three-and-a-half. Up to the age of seven, children form fewer long-term biographical memories than would be expected with normal forgetting. Freud called this phenomenon 'the remarkable amnesia of childhood' and saw it as evidence for his theory that infantile memories are actively blocked or repressed as part of psychosexual development.

Another theory is that, without language, young children cannot conceptualize in a form that can be recorded, but this does not explain why infantile amnesia is also found in animals, and is contradicted by studies showing that even newborns can learn and form memories. If the memories are being formed but are later not available, perhaps they are being wiped or overwritten. It is thought that in young animals, new cells are still being generated in episodic memory-crucial regions such as the hippocampus, and that this process of neurogenesis overwrites early memories. When neurogenesis slows down, long-term memories persist.

one who can see where the food is kept. They found that the chimps succeeded no more often than if they had been guessing randomly and concluded that they were not able to put themselves in the shoes of the blindfolded handler. They were only able to see things from their own point of view. In Piaget's model this might be said to correspond to the egocentric stage.

Theory of mind is a key concept in understanding the possible mechanism of autism, which is the name given to a condition that seems to involve failure of cognitive development along some key axes. Severely autistic children often fail the Sally-Anne test (see opposite), for example, even when they are older, suggesting that they may lack a theory of mind and suffer from a kind of 'mind-blindness'.

Being unable to conceptualize other minds makes social interactions extremely difficult, akin to trying to play tennis when the other side of the tennis court is invisible. By the same token, acquiring a theory of mind has an obvious adaptive value, allowing someone who has this ability to predict and manipulate others peoples' thoughts, feelings and behaviours – for instance, knowing when someone is lying, or how to tell a convincing lie – and may have been a crucial milestone in human cognitive evolution.

One theory of the evolution of intelligence, known as the 'Machiavellian intelligence hypothesis', is that intelligence evolved as a result of a feedback loop between social intelligence and increasing social complexity; theory

The Sally-Anne experiment

An elegant test of theory in mind (see above) in children is the Sally-Anne experiment, which relates to a child's ability to attribute false beliefs – to understand that someone else might hold a mistaken belief (and act accordingly), even when the child knows better. A child watches a little drama played out between two dolls, Sally and Anne. Anne watches Sally place a ball into a basket, but when Sally leaves, Anne moves the ball into a box. Sally then returns and wants to look for her ball, and the child is asked, 'Where will Sally look for the ball?' Children under three, like the chimps in Premack and Woodruff's study, cannot put themselves in the shoes of another and so assume that because they know where the ball is, Sally must also know, and so she will look in the box. Children of four and over, who have developed a theory of mind, will understand that Sally will have a false belief, and thus that she will look in the basket where she still believes the ball to be.

of mind would have been crucial to facilitate this. On a more positive note, theory of mind is also at the root of compassion and empathy, and thus underpins pro-social and cooperative behaviour.

Autism and Asperger's

Autism, deriving from the Greek for 'self', was a term first used in the early twentieth century to describe pathologically withdrawn schizophrenics. In 1943 the American child psychiatrist Leo Kanner (1894–1981) used the term 'early infantile autism' to describe a set of children who were highly intelligent but exhibited 'a powerful desire for aloneness' and 'an obsessive insistence on persistent sameness.' In 1944 the German scientist Hans Asperger (1906–80) first described his eponymous syndrome, in relation to highly intelligent children with obsessive interests and poor socialization.

Asperger's syndrome is now regarded as describing children nearer to the neurotypical end of a spectrum of autistic traits, with severe autism at the other end. Many aspects of the autism field are controversial, from the characterization and stigmatization of the condition, to the dramatic increase in diagnosis and apparent prevalence, to the possible causes. For instance, a once popular theory developed in the 1960s by the Austrian-American child psychologist Bruno Bettelheim (1903–90), now considered to be misogynistic and discredited, linked development of autism to emotionally cold and distant (so-called 'frigid') mothers.

Vygotsky, society and culture

Piaget's theory of intellectual development (see page 109) focuses on the individual and is universal, because it claims all children go through the same stages. An alternative, highly influential theory of cognitive development was developed by the Soviet psychologist Lev Vygotsky, at around the same time that Piaget was developing his theories in the 1920s and 1930s. His 'social developmental theory' emphasized the importance of society and culture, so that whereas Piaget's child developed almost in a vacuum, Vygotsky's child developed as the result of social inputs and in a culturally specific way. For Piaget, intellectual development preceded and enabled learning, but Vygotsky saw learning as triggering cognitive development.

Chomsky and being hardwired for speech

In Piaget's model (see page 111), language follows on from thought, with children first developing concepts and then learning the words for them. Vygotsky saw it the other way around, with cognitive skills developing independently of language at first but then getting a boost from the internalization of language to produce verbal thought, so that language acquisition drove cognitive development. But both models face the challenge of explaining the remarkable speed and facility with which very young children display language skills. For instance, speech patterns heard in the womb can be recognized by newborns, while infants less than a year old can parse language into word 'chunks' by using cues such as syllable stress. By the age of three most children have learned to understand and produce entirely new sentences, an ability that American linguist Noam Chomsky (b. 1928) called 'generative grammar'.

Chomksy's theory about language acquisition is nativist, in contrast to the empiricism of the behaviourist account that sees language acquisition as a process of imitation, repetition and reinforcement. Such mechanisms, he argued, were insufficient to explain how infants learn complex rules so quickly from what he described as a relatively impoverished linguistic context, i.e. the kind of baby talk adults use to communicate with infants. Chomsky believed that children are born equipped with some sort of hardwired cognitive module or tool, which he called the language acquisition device (LAD), built from genetically encoded Universal Grammar rules.

Chomsky's assertion about the quality of linguistic input children receive is now regarded as mistaken. It is believed that infants are exposed to a rich and nuanced stream of syntactical and semantic cues that scaffold their learning, so that it may not be necessary to posit some special language device.

Learning to read

The psychology of learning to read is especially interesting because it is a case where theory has profound consequences for application.

- The mainstream view of reading is that it involves learning to decode 'graphemes' (letter symbols or groups of letters) into phonemes (units of speech). This is the basis of the teaching style known as 'process-centred learning': a popular example of this is phonics, which seeks to give children a robust and easily replicable grounding in the rules of decoding.

- Decoding would be a lot more straightforward if language and spelling were more rational but they often are not (English is particularly full of exceptions).

- This means it is hard to specify a reliable set of rules, and it may be that learning to decode involves mastering 'probabilistic relationships' (rules of thumb about what is likely) rather than memorizing rules, in a similar way to learning a skill like catching a ball or riding a bicycle.

But there also seems to be another way in which some children learn to read, where they spontaneously learn to recognize whole words and their meaning, rather than sounding out phonemes that are devoid of meaning. Known as 'meaning-centred learning', this approach is demonstrated by a small percentage of children – 'precocious readers' – who seem to teach themselves to read by the age of four. The natural learning movement argues that all children should be encouraged to read in this way, as it is more enjoyable because it is more meaningful.

WHERE DOES GENDER COME FROM?

Gender, as opposed to sex, describes the roles and identities associated with males and females. Sex is biologically determined, but where does gender come from? The process by which an individual comes to identify with a socioculturally determined gender role (i.e. when they assume a gender role identity) is known as gender typing. Freud theorized that gender typing occurs when children identify with their same sex parent and internalize the associated qualities and characteristics. This positioned him on the nurture side of the debate over whether gender is rooted in nature or nurture.

Evolutionary biology argues that:

• Gender roles resulted from adaptive strategies that maximized reproductive success. So, for instance, men evolved aggression, risk-taking and philandering because their greatest chances of reproductive success lay in maximizing the number of partners (by fighting for access if necessary) and minimizing the resources spent on each.

- Meanwhile women evolved nurturing and compliance because they needed to maximize the resources and protection they could get from partners and provide for their offspring.

Behaviourist, social learning and social cognition theories, on the other hand, emphasize:

- Nurture – they see gender typing as the result of social influences, with gender-appropriate behaviour, reinforced and modelled.

- Especially dramatic examples of this come from anthropological studies. For instance, the Sakalavas people of Madagascar would raise 'pretty' boys as girls, and these children would adopt female gender roles. Similarly, the Aleutian Islanders in Alaska would raise handsome boys as girls, plucking their beards at puberty and marrying them to rich men. Again, these boys would, apparently, readily accept their reassigned gender role.

Non-binary gender identities

Both the Crow and Mojave Native American peoples recognize, or used to recognize, gender identities and roles beyond the traditional pair. Amongst the Crow, the term 'berdache' describes a male who opts not to follow the traditional warrior role, and who can even act as the 'wife' of a warrior, being recognized as such by his society. The Mojave people were said to recognize four gender roles, including *hwame*, a female who chose to live as a man, and *alyha*, a male who lived as a woman, even cutting his thigh to mimic menstruation and going through a ritual pregnancy.

ADOLESCENCE

According to the influential American psychologist and educationalist G. Stanley Hall (1846–1924) in his 1904 book *Adolescence,* adolescence is stereotypically a period of *sturm und drang* (storm and stress). And this idea helped create the popular western notion of adolescence as a distinct developmental stage of great promise and peril, during which physical changes and sexual urges must be carefully monitored, shaped and guided to prevent delinquency and amorality. Hall was greatly influenced by the psychoanalytic movement and its account of this stage of development, which would come to be known as the 'classical theory of adolescence'.

The classical theory of adolescence

According to influential post-Freudians, such as Erik Erikson (1902–94) and Peter Blos (1904–97), adolescence is a time of inner conflict and potentially difficult or traumatic psychic and personality realignment. In Erikson's psychosocial theory, the crisis of adolescence is a conflict between identity and role confusion: 'At no other phase of the life cycle are the pressures of finding oneself and the threat of losing oneself so closely allied.'

In order to resolve this, young people must establish a sense of self-identity and a 'feeling of being at home in one's body, a sense of knowing where one is going and an inner assurance of anticipated recognition from those who count.' The reward for success, Erikson said, is fidelity; finding an identity to which one can be true while accepting other people's differences.

Blos, the post-war German-American child psychoanalyst (known as 'Mr Adolescence' for his work with teenagers), called this quest for self-identity a 'second individuation process', the first having taken place in childhood. Processes involved include:

• Disengagement from the family unit as the young person seeks an independent identity, leading to regression, where substitute parental figures are sought through hero worship (of pop idols, for instance).

- Regression to ambivalence, where adolescents are simultaneously drawn to and reject parental attachment and approval. In seeking to escape dependence, the adolescent may exhibit negative dependence, where behaviour is dictated by the urge to do the opposite of what parents want.

- Blos saw regression and its consequences as adaptive responses that help prevent the adolescent from maintaining dependence, and which are thus necessary for establishing independence.

This view of adolescence as time of strife and disturbance may not be the whole picture. Most young people have positive relations with their parents and negotiate adolescence relatively smoothly.

Inventing adolescence

Adolescence is widely viewed in social psychology as a largely socio-culturally constructed phenomenon. Up until relatively recently most young people were expected to transition into adult roles as soon as they were able, driven by economic necessity, while in many traditional and pre-industrial cultures rites of passage, such as circumcision or ritual seclusion, were used to mark a clear and abrupt transition from childhood to adulthood. It is only in the modern era that there is an extended period during which young people are economically and socially dependent during, and beyond, physical and sexual maturation. This has been interpreted as being something which is likely to lead to inevitable conflict between roles, demands and urges.

6

What you need to know about

AGEING

Shakespeare wrote that 'one man in his time plays many parts', and went on to list the seven ages of man. The mewling, puking infant and whining school-boy are considered in the previous chapter; about the subsequent five ages the bard had some pointed psychological insights. The soldier is 'jealous in honour ... seeking the bubble reputation, even in the cannon's mouth', while the justice is 'full of wise saws' and the very old man sinks into 'second childishness and mere oblivion'.

POST-FREUDIAN STAGES OF ADULTHOOD

Developmental and geriatric psychology offer their own approaches to the ages of man and woman, with observations on the causes and effects of stress, the cognitive effects of decline and the changing pattern of social connections in the course of life.

The most obvious parallel that psychology offers to Shakespeare is Erikson's 'Eight Ages of Man' model. Erik Erikson was a German art student and teacher who fell into Freud's orbit and went on to become a highly influential psychoanalyst. In the 1930s and 1940s, he helped develop a post-Freudian, more humanistic approach to psychodynamics called 'ego psychology', which viewed the ego as having the capacity to be autonomous and dynamic, and considered its lifelong development to be an interaction with its social and physical environment, rather than being locked in to patterns and complexes fixed in childhood.

Erikson went on to develop his psychosocial theory of the Eight Ages, an account of the different challenges and tasks that humans face. At each stage the individual is confronted with specific conflicts that are either successfully resolved, leading to growth and the acquisition of 'virtues' (positive attributes), or not, in which case psychic damage and vices might result.

From adolescence to middle age, Erikson said that people face a conflict between intimacy and isolation: should the individual risk pain by opening themselves up to others? The potential reward is the virtue of love, but failure can lead to loneliness and depression. In their middle years (between forty and sixty-five), people face the challenge of achieving 'generativity', i.e. giving back to the world through creativity or nurturing, such as success at work, making a home, or pursuing hobbies – and avoiding stagnation. Success leads to feeling connected, involved and worthy, leading to the virtue Erikson called 'care', while stagnation leaves the individual feeling unproductive and alienated.

Erikson characterized the final stage as a conflict between ego integrity and despair, describing the former as 'the acceptance of one's one and only life cycle as something that had to be' with 'a sense of coherence and wholeness'. The alternative is to face death feeling unhappy with your life when it is too late to do anything about it, and feeling that life was not worthwhile and lacked meaning. Successfully overcoming despair could lead to the virtue of wisdom.

The psychosocial stages

Stage	Psychosocial Crisis	Basic Virtue	Existential Question	Age
1	Trust v Mistrust	Hope	Can I trust the world?	0 – 1½
2	Autonomy v Shame	Will	Is it OK to be me?	1½ - 3
3	Initiative v Guilt	Purpose	Is it okay for me to do, move and act?	3-5
4	Industry v Inferiority	Competency	Can I make it in the world of people and things?	5-12
5	Identity v Role Confusion	Fidelity	Who am I? Who can I be?	12-18
6	Intimacy v Isolation	Love	Can I love?	18 – 40
7	Generativity v Stagnation	Care	Can I make my life count?	40 – 65
8	Ego Integrity v Despair	Wisdom	Is it okay to have been me?	65

Erikson's model talks in sweeping terms about existential challenges, but life throws up plenty of other problems, from the serious to the mundane. What effects do these have on the psyche? The link between stress and health – both mental and physical – is now well established. There is even a branch of psychology called psychoneuroimmunology, which looks at the links between neurology and the immune system. One of the best known and most widely used tools for exploring this issue is the 1960s Social Readjustment

Laughter therapy

A dramatic illustration of the potential for psychological interventions to impact on health and potentially treat disease is the example of laughter therapy, which first secured mainstream medical attention with the 1964 publication of *Anatomy of an Illness* by Norman Cousins (1915–90). He details his self-treatment of a painful and apparently difficult and incurable condition. When doctors appeared unable to do much for him, Cousins checked himself out of hospital and into a hotel room and watched comedy films and TV, such as the Marx Brothers and *Candid Camera*. He found that laughter alleviated his pain and allowed him to sleep. Other evidence suggests that laughter can indeed have direct positive effects on the immune system.

Rating Scale (SRRS), also known as the 'Holmes and Rahe stress scale', after its creators, the American psychiatrists Thomas Holmes and Richard Rahe.

Everyday hassles and uplifts

Inspired by a poem by Charles Bukowski (1920–94), which points out that 'It's not the large things that send a man to the madhouse . . . it's the continuing series of small tragedies', the American psychologist Allen Kanner and colleagues explored the effects of minor events on health. They designed a 117 item 'Hassles scale', which asks people to rate stress caused by day-to-day anxieties and problems, from money woes to traffic jams, marital arguments to job disappointments and body image to bad luck. They described daily hassles as 'irritating, frustrating, distressing demands that to some degree characterize everyday transactions with the environment'. Items on the scale include:

- Not enough time for family.

- Not enough money for entertainment or recreation.

- Gossip.

- Job dissatisfactions.

- Filling out forms.

Recognizing that positive emotions can boost health, they also compiled an inventory of 135 items which they called 'uplifts' such as:

- Doing volunteer work.

- Liking fellow workers.

- Finding something presumed lost.

- Being efficient.

- Eating out.

- Buying things for the house.

Kanner and his team found that the five most common hassles concerned weight, the health of a family member, rising prices of common goods, home maintenance and having too many things to do. The five most common uplifts were relating well with a spouse or lover, relating well with friends, completing a task, feeling healthy and getting enough sleep.

When hassles and uplifts scores were correlated with mental health symptoms, the researchers found that their hassle scale was a more accurate predictor of stress-related problems, such as anxiety and depression, than the SRRS. Hassles were also a better predictor of well-being than uplifts. Uplifts were shown to have a positive effect on the stress levels of women, but not men. Kanner explained these effects through two mechanisms: 'accumulation', where constant small stressors build up to give a greater stress response; and 'amplification', where a more serious source of stress magnifies the effect of minor hassles.

The ageing brain

Neurogenesis (production of new nerve cells) is largely complete by the end of adolescence, and from this period on the ageing brain experiences a net loss of neurons. The list goes on:

- By late adulthood you are losing more than 100,000 nerve cells a day. Compared to the total (c. 100 billion) this is a small proportion, but by the age of eighty to ninety up to 40 per cent of cortical cells may have been lost. Also, the cortex gets thinner and fluid-filled spaces called ventricles enlarge slightly. However, neither of these changes actually affects brain power very much.

- More serious is the decline in blood supply to the brain, which can slow it down and make it vulnerable to blood clots (causing strokes).

- The brain also becomes more vulnerable to degenerative diseases such as Alzheimer's, where plaques of protein build up around some neurons interfering

with their function and reducing the density of connections they can make.

These bare facts of biology have driven the development of
the decrement model of the psychology of ageing, which
views ageing as a period of decline. But is the picture this
straightforward?

Does intelligence decline with age?

Research with a battery of IQ and other cognitive tests has shown
that there is no uniform pattern of age-related change across
the spectrum of intellectual abilities. According to the American psychologist K. Warner Schaie (b. 1928), one of the leading
experts in the field and the founder of the mid-twentieth
century Seattle Longitudinal Study (SLS), this means that:

- IQ tests are 'insufficient to monitor age changes ... in
  intellectual functioning'.

- A more nuanced approach is necessary, which
  recognizes the extent to which cognitive abilities are
  conserved into old age.

- There are no clear signs of overall cognitive decline in
  the population before the age of sixty and, although
  decline is observable in most functions of people
  aged seventy-four and over, when researchers follow

The Mankato nuns

One famous study illustrates that even the very old can retain mental sharpness. In the Mankato Nun Study, a group of elderly nuns from the convent of the School Sisters of Notre Dame on Good Counsel Hill in Mankato, Minnesota, underwent a variety of tests, and also comparisons with material they had produced when they were much younger. Many of the Sisters had reached ripe old ages – some were over 100. The research showed, among other things, that it is possible to maintain mental agility and sharpness up to and beyond the age of 100. Many of the elderly nuns scored just as high as ever in tests and displayed their mental acuity in their daily lives, through their activities in learning and teaching, reading and debating, and engaging in mentally challenging leisure pursuits such as crosswords and puzzles.

an individual's performance through life, even at the age of eighty-one, less than half of individuals show significant decline in the preceding seven years.

Schaie's work with the SLS, which began in 1956 and tracked the psychological development over fifty years of around 6000 people of all age groups, led the American and Canadian governments to raise the retirement age for many professions in recognition of the evidence about maintenance of cognitive abilities.

Physical, mental and social factors also contribute to the maintenance of cognitive abilities:

- Aerobic fitness and the absence of cardiovascular or other chronic disease are important. According to Waneen Spirduso (b. 1936), director of the Institute of Gerontology at the University of Texas in Austin, the two factors that best predict an older person's performance in tests of mental agility are the number of years the person has exercised in the past and the person's current aerobic capacity.

- Social factors include higher socio-economic status; enjoying a complex and stimulating environment and lifestyle; and having a partner who also maintains their cognitive status.

- Personality has also been shown to correlate with the conservation of cognitive function; those who are more flexible in their approach to life will maintain their cognition better.

- The status of a person's perceptual abilities also has a major impact − maintaining hearing and vision, for instance, are associated with better cognition.

Does memory get worse?

As with intelligence, the story of how memory changes with age is nuanced. Long-term memory does show decline in old age, which is mainly linked to retrieval. Up until very advanced ages, however, working memory remains largely unaffected in pure tests such as digit-span but it suffers in tasks that require divided attention, such as dichotic listening, where different sounds are played to each ear). This may relate to the 'plasticity and stability dilemma'.

Plasticity is the ability of the brain to rewire itself, either through growing new neurons or making new connections between existing ones. Plasticity explains how, for instance, brains can recover from damage or amputees can learn to control prosthetics. Plasticity is key to all types of learning.

- Traditionally, it was believed that plasticity is reserved for young brains, but in fact this is not the case.

- According to Kurt Fischer (b. 1943), education professor and director of the Mind, Brain, and Education Program at Harvard University, 'The brain is remarkably plastic. Even in middle or old age, it's still adapting very actively to its environment.'

- Cognitive neuroscientist Patricia Reuter-Lorenz of the University of Michigan in Ann Arbor points to the brain's 'enduring potential for plasticity, reorganization and preservation of capacities'. This means that older people can be highly effective in learning new information and skills. For instance, in a 2007 study in the journal *Neurology*, pilots aged forty to sixty-nine, tested on new flight simulators, proved to be more successful at avoiding collisions than younger pilots, although it took them longer to learn to use the simulators.

What can impair learning in older people, however, is what cognitive scientists call stability: the ability of a learning system to remain stable in response to irrelevant input. Older people have less stable learning systems that are more easily disturbed by distraction and interference. In 2014, a Brown University study showed how the good performance of older people, given a visual perception task, was masked by instability as they failed to filter out stimuli that were irrelevant.

Professor Takeo Watanabe, lead author of the study, pointed out that 'Plasticity may be kept OK ... [but] we have found that the stability is problematic. Our learning and memory capability is limited. You don't want older, existing important information that is already stored to be replaced with trivial information.' Studies such as these suggest that older people's learning might be improved with training to help them filter out confounding inputs more effectively.

Friends and family

As well as the kind of intrapersonal changes Erikson outlined in his psychosocial theory (see page 128), interpersonal psychology is also not static over time. The way in which people relate to friends and family changes with age and has significant consequences for mental and physical health.

The key finding from social psychological surveys of ageing is that the number of social partners (which covers acquaintances, friends and family) declines with age. Specifically, the number of peripheral partners declines, but this is matched by a more intense focus on close social partners. In other words, older people tend to have fewer but deeper friendships and relations, pruning more casual acquaintances. This finding is consistent across different ethnicities and cultures.

This increased focus on core relationships brings psychological benefits. People report that satisfaction with close friends and family members increases with age. In particular marital satisfaction increases into old age. And good relationships bring mental health benefits; for instance, positive sibling relationships have been shown to correlate with lower rates of depression, and there is also a strong correlation between marital status and happiness in old age (married people tend to be happier than single ones).

Maintaining meaningful relationships into old age is also associated with handling stress better, getting ill less and recovering more quickly, and a decreased risk of mortality. Moreover, it is correlated with lower rates of depression, anxiety and sleep disturbance. Not all close relationships are beneficial, however; for older people caregiving relationships, are generally (though not universally) negatively correlated with well-being, reflecting the stress and demands of such roles.

7

What you need to know about
MENTAL ILLNESS

The study and treatment of mental illness is hedged about with jargon, with terms that are often confusing because they differ in nuanced ways. For instance, the scientific study of mental illness is known as abnormal psychology – begging the question, what is 'normal'? – or psychopathology, and must be distinguished from clinical psychology, the professional branch of psychology that deals with mental illness.

Both abnormal and clinical psychology study the nature, origin, diagnosis, classification, treatment and prevention of mental disorders and disabilities but the former does so from a scientific/academic approach and the latter from a healthcare/treatment approach. Clinical psychology is also not to be confused with psychiatry, the branch of medicine concerned with mental illness, although the differences are mainly ones of training and statutory powers (e.g. a psychiatrist is a medical doctor who specializes in mental health). To some extent these different terms reflect the history of mental illness and its study and treatment.

MENTAL ILLNESS IN HISTORY

The earliest evidence that might tell us something about the medical treatment of mental disorders, and therefore of their existence, comes from prehistoric skulls with holes drilled in them. This is known as trepanning or trephination, and is still practised by some eccentrics today. It was apparently relatively common – or at least well established – in pre-historic times, given the geographical range across which it occurred, and the skill with which it was done. Trepanning was most likely used to treat swelling on the brain caused by head injuries, but it may also indicate prehistoric attribution of mental disorder to some qualities of or entities in the brain, such as the belief that madness is caused by evil spirits, and the desire to free them through a hole in the head.

Ancient accounts of madness

Biblical and mythical sources record the belief that mental illness might be supernatural in origin, as in the Biblical account of the madness of King Saul, who is 'troubled by an evil spirit from God', or the madness inflicted on Hercules by the goddess Hera. But contrary to popular belief, pre-scientific cultures were not ignorant of biological or psychological causes of mental illness, and from ancient times there is clear

Dream temples

Magic and mysticism mixed with psychological medicine in the practice of dream therapy, which took place in institutions dedicated to this practice. At temples sacred to the legendary healer Asclepius, god of medicine, patients would pray for healing dreams before going to sleep in the *abaton*, a subterranean precinct set aside for the purpose. Specific classes of mental disorder were treated at different temples: the temple at Megara treated emotional disturbances, the temple in Epidaurus specialized in mental illness associated with the blood of Medusa and the temple at Tricca was for hysterics.

evidence that physicians sought rational, natural explanations. There was also a considerable amount of crossover.

For instance, in the ancient Greek legend of Iphiclus (an Argonaut who suffered from infertility or impotence, depending on the source), the legendary healer Melampus employs a kind of proto-Freudian analysis. Iphiclus' affliction is deemed to be at least partly psychogenic (caused by psychological factors), with Melampus tracing his disorder to a childhood incident in which Iphiclus is frightened by the sight of his father brandishing a bloody knife. Magic enters the picture, however, because the cure involves a potion made of rust taken from the offending blade.

Ancient diagnosis and therapy

The Greek physician Hippocrates (*c.* 460–*c.* 375 BC) clearly attributed mental disorders to natural causes, linked to the brain. He advocated a holistic approach to medicine, seeing mental disturbances as being linked to personality and mood, as well as disturbances in bodily fluids. Hippocrates spoke of 'humours' (see page 66), whereas a modern physician might speak of neurotransmitters or neuroendocrines. The Graeco-Roman physician Galen (130–210) recognized that mental illness could have organic causes, such as head injuries or alcohol, and psychological ones, such as grief or stress.

When it came to diagnosis, the Ancient Greeks and Romans recognized a set of conditions which were not so different from modern diagnoses, including:

- Melancholia, similar to the modern diagnosis of depression; dementia; mania, including symptoms such as frenzy and euphoria; and hysteria, similar to modern conversion disorder, in which psychological distress is manifested as physical symptoms (e.g. hysterical blindness).

- Like modern psychologists, they also drew a distinction between delusions (false beliefs) and hallucinations (seeing, hearing and otherwise sensing things that aren't there).

- The Roman statesman and philosopher Cicero (106–43 BC) even designed a questionnaire to aid in the assessment of mental illness. It included questions on *habitus* (appearance), *orationes* (speech) and *casus* (significant life events – recalling the SRRS inventory; see page 131).

- Many of the treatments they used were humane and sensitive. For instance, Hippocrates prescribed quiet living, healthy diet and exercise, and later Greek and Roman physicians recommended music, massage and baths.

Medieval madness

Into early modern times, most mentally ill people would have remained in their communities, reliant on their family for care. But from medieval times there were institutions that became associated with housing the insane. These asylums, of which the infamous Bedlam (actually the Bethlem Hospital) was the archetype, were not initially intended for long-term incarceration of patients. The records of Bethlem show that most of those who passed through its doors would expect to return home in weeks or months, although a list of patients from 1598 indicates that at least one woman had been there for twenty-five years.

Medieval authorities recognized natural, rational causes for insanity, known as 'idiocy'. According to the medieval historian David Roffe, 'Madness was overwhelmingly perceived as a disorder of the body and brain'. Inquests to determine causes of death indicated, whenever possible, natural or physical ones. In 1309, for instance, an inquest found that Bartholemew de Sakeville had become an idiot after developing an acute fever, while in 1349 Robert de Irthlingborough's memory loss and subsequent idiocy were linked to a blow to the head he received from a lance while jousting.

Treatments for mental illness were limited at best, extending to what Roffe calls 'the typical dietary, herbal, and surgical regimes of classical medicine'. The aim of such treatment was to rebalance essential qualities, such as heat or dryness, and they used different foods and herbs, particularly spices, believed to have relevant qualities of their own. So, dietary treatments included extensive use of pepper, cumin, cardamom, cinnamon and cloves, while the surgical regime was mainly limited to bleeding by cutting or leeching (which was believed to drain off excess humours and thus rebalance the person's system). Meanwhile, unfortunate inmates at places like Bedlam were simply confined in chains.

Bedlam

Bedlam became the popular name for a hospital in London actually called Bethlem. Originally it was a priory for knights (a kind of religious hostel), founded in 1247 and attached to the Church of St Mary of Bethlehem, hence the name. By 1329 it was being used as a hospital, where shelter, food and the most basic of care were provided to homeless and sick people, including the mentally ill. By 1403 it was home to insane people from across England, whose families could not care for them.

In 1547 Henry VIII gifted Bethlem Hospital to the City of London and it became the first and only public mental institution in England, a distinction it would hold until well into the 1800s. In 1676 it moved to a large new building, with a baroque facade designed by the natural philosopher Robert Hooke. Over the following century it became synonymous with chaos and 'raving lunatics', and people began to visit it for entertainment. A travelling German scholar, Von Uffenbach, recorded that he visited in 1710 hoping to see a patient who 'crowed all day long like a cock', but was redirected by the staff to visit instead 'the most foolish and ludicrous of all ... [an inmate who] imagined that he was a Captain and wore a wooden sword at his side and had severall cock's feathers stuck into his hat. He wanted to command the others and did all kinds of tomfoolery.' Public visits were finally banned in 1770, and the site of the hospital is now on the southern fringe of London where it still exists today.

Alienists and psychiatrists

By around 1800 physicians who specialized in mental ill-ness were generally known as 'alienists', because they dealt with disorders of 'mental alienation'. The term 'psychiatrist' would not take over from alienist for around a century, during which developments in Paris, the centre of research and practice in this field, would dramatically change the theory and practice of psychiatry. The focus for these developments was La Salpêtrière, a hospital where Jean-Martin Charcot (1825–93) had been made a professor of pathological anatomy. At this time alienists/psychiatrists firmly located the causes of mental illnesses in the matter of the brain, believing that disorders such as schizophrenia and psychotic depression had similar roots to those such as Parkinson's disease, being caused by lesions in the brain.

Charcot initially insisted that he had no interest in mental medicine but through his work on hysterics (women who exhibited neurotic symptoms alongside apparently physical and neurological ones) he practically created the new field of neurology, the study of disorders of the nervous system. Because he was not an alienist, he was open to new approaches to understanding hysteria and other mental illness, and he inspired a new generation of physicians, including Freud and the French philosopher and psychology pioneer Pierre Janet, to develop psychological explanations. Jung later wrote of his dissatisfaction with the prevailing biological model of the alienists. '"Mental

The Rosenhan study

In 1973 the journal *Science* published a bombshell study, 'On being sane in insane places' by Stanford University psychologist David Rosenhan (1929–2012). In order to evaluate clinical psychiatric practice, Rosenhan had sent volunteers, who had claimed to have experienced auditory hallucinations to get themselves admitted and diagnosed with psychiatric disorders, to several psychiatric institutions. Once admitted, the volunteers behaved normally and told staff that they felt fine, but none were allowed to leave without confessing to having a mental illness and agreeing to take medication as a condition of release. When a hospital objected to the study and challenged Rosenhan to send volunteers, he agreed. Out of 250 new patients in the following weeks, the hospital reported over forty suspected 'pseudopatients'; in fact Rosenhan had not sent any.

diseases are diseases of the brain" was the axiom, and told one just nothing at all.'

Through their work with Charcot and his team, Freud and Janet came to focus on the psychology of mental illness, rather than its physiology or neurology. Ironically, neurology had helped create psychoanalysis and depth psychology. From now on psychiatrists would increasingly focus on the psychological causes and treatment of mental illness.

CHEMICAL SOLUTIONS

Psychoanalysis and similar psychotherapy techniques became the dominant paradigm in psychiatry, but talking therapies proved largely ineffective in the treatment of the most severe mental illnesses, the psychoses, and their characteristic symptoms of delusion, hallucination and depression. Sufferers of conditions like schizophrenia, bipolar disease and psychotic depression were condemned to be locked away in asylums where the best to be hoped was that they would be managed and prevented from causing harm to themselves and others.

This would all change in the 1940s with the development of psychiatric drugs, beginning with neuroleptics, a class of antipsychotic medicine that, for the first time, offered a degree of control over florid symptoms such as hallucination and delusion. Other drug treatments followed, including antidepressants and anxiolytics for treating anxiety. Drug therapy revolutionized psychiatric medicine, making it possible for many previously intractable patients to leave hospital, and those with milder conditions to live something approaching a normal life. They also saved thousands of lives by preventing suicide.

Psychiatric drugs, however, can have severe side effects and this was especially true in the early days of their development. Over-prescription and poor practice, particularly in large and often hard-pressed psychiatric hospitals, led to the growth of an increasingly vocal anti-psychiatry movement. Revelations of failures in diagnosis and public antipathy to practices such as electroconvulsive therapy (ECT) were exacerbated by the popularity of the 1975 film *One Flew Over the Cuckoo's Nest*.

Prozac

The early antidepressants belonged to classes called mono-amine oxidase inhibitors (MAOIs) and tricyclics. They help boost levels in the brain of the neurotransmitters norepi-nephrine and serotonin. Their effects were dramatic; they saved lives and bought sufferers time to implement proper treatment. They can help restore sleep patterns, appetite and energy, and they made it easier for patients to focus on their problems and avoid institutionalization. But their side effects, both mental and physical, can be severe: dry mouth, headaches, constipation, nausea, blurred vision, confusion, weight gain and delayed ejaculation/orgasm.

In 1987 a new antidepressant called fluoxetine (trade name Prozac) came onto the market. Prozac is a selective serotonin reuptake inhibitor (SSRI), which specifically targets just one neurotransmitter. It has fewer side effects than other antidepressants and is highly effective. It soon became the best-selling antidepressant of all time. In the initial years after its launch Prozac was hailed as a wonder drug, gaining reams of publicity and support. Soon people who would never normally dream of taking drugs for a mood disorder were asking for Prozac by name. But what happened and why?

- Inevitably there was a backlash. In practice Prozac is not a miracle cure for depression – it is effective at relieving the symptoms of depression in between 60 and 80 per cent of users, a similar success rate to other antidepressants.

- Like other antidepressants it has side effects, particularly on sexual function, and many users complain that while Prozac evens out troughs in mood, it also prevents peaks.

- Growing fears of over-prescription (and the over-diagnosis of depression), together with scare stories linking it to violent outbursts and suicides, raised concerns about the original testing procedures and the safety of the drug, though it is still commonly prescribed for bulimia, anxiety disorders and some forms of behavioural disorder in children.

And did you know?

- More than one in ten Americans over the age of 12 take antidepressants, with over 254 million prescriptions written in America in 2010.

- They are the second most prescribed class of drug in medicine.

And all this is despite the fact that there is no real understanding of how or why they work, and no proof that problems like depression are actually caused by chemical imbalances in the brain. Many psychology health professionals argue that their field has become 'too biological', with a dogmatic focus on physiological aspects of mental illness that may not even exist, while insufficient attention is paid to the psychological, social and spiritual aspects of mental health.

DEFINING MENTAL ILLNESS

The anti-psychiatry movement argues that many psychiatric definitions are arbitrary and invalid, labels affixed to loose constellations of symptoms in order to pathologize behaviour that falls outside narrowly defined bands of 'normality'. In fact the term 'abnormal psychology' itself begs the question of what constitutes normality. This question is central to the theory and practice of mental healthcare and has massive impact on individuals and society.

The four D's

There is no single arbiter of normality, or 'neurotypicality', but the generally agreed criteria are the four D's: deviance, distress, dysfunction and danger. All of them can be controversial, subject to interpretation and dependent on context.

- Deviance refers to thoughts and behaviour deemed to deviate from social norms, and is perhaps inevitably the most fraught criteria. Social norms change and are not necessarily congruent with morality, let alone historical perspective. In the context of abnormal psychology, homosexuality is one of the classic examples. In Europe and America homosexuality was classed as deviance until relatively recently, and it still is in many parts of the world. In the 1950s and 1960s homosexuality was treated with controversial aversion therapy, and some groups still advocate such methods today.

- Distress refers to subjective harms caused by thoughts and behaviours. Such harms are highly context-dependent; for instance, self-harm is a feature of many religious rites, while those who engage in extreme high-risk sports can be reckless for fun. Conversely a mental disorder such as mania can cause euphoria even while being objectively harmful.

- Dysfunction refers to a person's ability to maintain 'normal' life, and whether their symptoms impact their cognition and behaviour to disrupt, for instance, their employment or family life.

- Danger, meaning whether someone poses a danger to themselves or others, is the ultimate arbiter of abnormality, but in fact mental illness rarely reaches this bar, limiting the utility of this criterion.

Borderline cases put the four-D system under special stress. Potentially extreme and invasive interventions could be triggered by decisions about which side of the line an individual stands. Critics argue that the system, or at least the way in which it is interpreted, incorrectly pathologizes non-conformists who may not pose any threat and do not really need treatment.

The Diagnostic Statistical Manual of Mental Disorders

Published by the American Psychiatric Association and known as the 'DSM', this manual was introduced in 2013 and is now in its fifth edition. It is of critical importance to both the day-to-day practice of psychiatry and psychotherapy in the US and the many other parts of the world that take their lead from it, and to psychology as a whole. In its own words the DSM is a 'critical resource for clinical practice', used 'to diagnose and classify mental disorders' and is 'intended to facilitate an objective assessment of symptom presentations in a variety of clinical settings ...' With concise checklists, its aim is to help psychologists, psychiatrists, social workers and others maintain consistent diagnosis and treatment.

Aversion therapy

Based on the behaviourist logic of simple conditioning, aversion therapy seeks to condition the subject to associate a target cognition, attitude or behaviour with negative stimuli, by repeatedly presenting them in concert. This is the rationale behind the drug Antabuse (disulfuram), a drug that produces nausea and other unpleasant reactions when alcohol is drunk, in order to condition someone to dislike alcohol.

Aversion therapy to 'treat' homosexuality was used up until the 1960s. In one example from 1935 a man was given electric shocks while he imagined homoerotic fantasies, and a 1963 trial in which a man stood barefoot on an electrified metal floor and was shocked while being shown pictures of naked men was reported to have turned the subject bisexual after 4000 shocks. In 1964 a British man was killed by chemical aversion therapy that involved both negative reinforcement (nauseating drugs in conjunction with discussion of homosexuality), and supposedly positive (LSD in conjunction with heterosexual fantasizing).

The DSM can trace its roots back to nineteenth-century US censuses, which gathered data initially on 'idiocy/insanity' and, by 1880, on seven categories of mental health: mania, melancholia, monomania, paresis, dementia, dipsomania and epilepsy. In the 1920s the newly named American Psychiatric Association adopted the WHO's classification scheme, and after 1945 it reworked this to produce the first DSM, published in 1952. At this time disorders were known as 'reactions'.

Diagnostic inflation and exuberance

The DSM has become the focal point of many controversies, particularly the way in which the number of recognized disorders has ballooned, and its statistics have been blamed for the massive rise in the incidence – or at least diagnosis – of psychiatric illness in the western world since the Second World War. In the UK, for instance, in the fifty years after 1945, rates of psychiatric referral increased sixfold, while in the US the rate of diagnosis of bipolar disorder in young people increased 4000 per cent from 1994–2003.

The DSM is also accused of pathologizing normal emotions and behaviour, which means labelling them (even grief) as disorders, and of having been responsible for an irresponsible ballooning of diagnosis and thus of unnecessary medication. Robert Spitzer (1932–2015), who led the revision that created DSM-III, estimated that 20–30 per cent of cases that received a medical diagnosis as a result of the DSM might be 'normal reactions, which are not really disorders'. Dr Allen Frances (b. 1942), who chaired the DSM-IV Task Force, warned that temper tantrums might be labelled as 'disruptive mood dysregulation disorder' and normal forgetfulness in old age as 'mild neurocognitive disorder', while poor concentration is mislabelled as 'adult attention deficit hyperactity disorder'.

Eccentricity or madness?

Imagine that you are a psychiatrist deciding whether to admit a patient who has the following characteristics: nonconformism, creativity, extreme curiosity, idealism, obsessive interest in a hobby, awareness since childhood of being different, intelligence, outspokenness, lack of competitiveness, peculiar dietary habits, anti-social behaviour, mischievousness, lack of attachments, no siblings and poor spelling. Such a constellation of traits would generally mark someone out as deviant and potentially dysfunctional, though not dangerous or distressed. Should such an individual be offered drug or talking therapy? All of these characteristics come from an eccentricity checklist drawn up by David Weeks, author of a landmark 1995 study on eccentrics. He estimated that about 1 in 5,000 people is a 'classic eccentric'.

MAJOR MENTAL ILLNESSES

As we've seen, mainstream psychiatry in the west recognizes at least 300 disorders. These can be loosely categorized into three major classes – neurological conditions, psychoses, and personality disorders with anxiety and neuroses.

Neurological conditions

These affect the nervous system. The US National Institute for Neurological Disorders and Stroke lists 445 neurological disorders including developmental defects (such as spina bifida), infections (e.g. encephalitis), cancer (e.g. glioma), stroke, genetic conditions (cerebellar ataxia), degenerative disorders (e.g. Alzheimer's disease) and neuronal misfiring (epilepsy). There are also those with psychological components (e.g. attention-deficit-hyperactivity disorder) and those with physiological causes but higher order cognitive deficits (e.g. aphasia and amnesia).

Particularly interesting are those that link brain damage to specific cognitive functions. Classic examples include aphasia, agnosia and amnesia.

- Aphasia is where damage to parts of the brain, such as Wernicke's area, produces characteristic symptoms like 'word salad', a jumble of words that sounds like real language but which is actually devoid of meaning).

Anterograde amnesia

Anterograde amnesia is a rare form of the disorder characterized by the loss of the ability to form new memories. Short-term memory (STM) functions properly, but problems of storage or retrieval prevent the sufferer from making a permanent record of new information. An anterograde amnesiac could meet someone in the morning and spend several hours with them but would have no recollection of them by the afternoon.

Anterograde amnesia occurs because of oxygen deprivation through barbiturate overdose and discrete brain damage by piercing. It is one of the most common causes of Korsakoff's syndrome, a problem affecting alcoholics, where dietary patterns and drinking cause thiamin deficiency, leading in turn to the destruction of parts of the limbic system called the mamillary bodies. Stabilized Korsakoff's syndrome is characterized by anterograde amnesia accompanied by confabulation – where the sufferer invents explanations to explain the gaps in memory.

Intriguingly, anterograde amnesia usually affects only declarative memory (memory for facts, events, etc., sometimes described as 'knowing that'), while preserving procedural memory (memory for skills and procedures, sometimes described as 'knowing how'). Anterograde amnesiacs, for instance, can learn a new skill, but will not be able to say how they learned it.

- Agnosia is where the link between perception and recognition/comprehension is disturbed, as in the case that gave American neurologist Oliver Sacks (1933–2015) the title for his bestselling 1985 book *The Man Who Mistook His Wife For a Hat*, or in people suffering from prosopagnosia, who cannot recognize the face of a loved one and have to wait for them to speak to work out who they are.

- Amnesia is where the formation or recall of memories is disturbed. Complete, abrupt amnesia of the sort often depicted in movies – known as global amnesia – is extremely rare. An injury or insult to the brain, such as concussion, will often result in loss of memory for the immediate past. Conditions such as Korsakoff's syndrome (see anterograde amnesia, opposite) can result in bizarre forms of amnesia.

Psychoses

The strictest definition of a psychosis is a disorder in which the sufferer lacks insight into their condition (i.e. cannot distinguish fantasy from reality). More generally it is a disorder characterized by hallucinations and/or delusions. In psychiatry the psychoses are usually understood to be either 'organic' (typically degenerative diseases caused by brain damage from, for example, drinking or ageing) or 'functional' (the class that includes schizophrenia, bipolar disorder

– formerly known as manic-depression – and major depressive disorder).

Schizophrenia is characterized by:

- Negative symptoms, such as flat affect (lack of emotional expression), poverty of thought and speech and lack of purposiveness.

- Positive symptoms, such as delusions, hallucinations, hearing voices, disorganized speech, disorganized thinking and catatonia (remaining motionless in a stupor).

Bipolar disorder is characterized by:

- Wild swings of mood, with …

- Manic phases marked by euphoria, insomnia, poor judgement and delusions, and depressive episodes.

Major depressive disorders involve symptoms such as:

- Depressed mood, sleep disturbances, appetite loss, fatigue and intrusive (and sometimes suicidal) thoughts.

Whether or not psychotic disorders are discrete diseases with specific physiological causes is controversial; if such causes do exist they are unknown, and critics contend that these conditions are simply labels given to constellations of symptoms, which may or may not benefit from being treated together.

Delusions

These fixed beliefs do not match reality, deviate from cultural norms and are resistant to reason. They can be disabling and profoundly distressing, and can trigger deleterious and dangerous behaviour. Delusions are a characteristic symptom of schizophrenia, which often features some or all of: delusions of persecution (someone is out to get you), delusions of reference (you are the subject of signals that cannot really relate to you, such as radio broadcasts or overheard conversations between strangers) and delusions of control (some external influence is controlling your thoughts and actions).

Delusions can also feature in a range of other conditions such as dementia and depression, where nihilistic delusions, such as worthlessness, are common. Capgras syndrome is the delusion that people close to you have been replaced by lookalike impostors, while Fregoli syndrome, named after a famous quick-change artist, is the delusion that multiple different people are actually one person constantly changing their disguise or appearance.

Dissociative disorders

These are a complex, poorly understood and controversial set of psychiatric disorders involving dissociation, a sense of disconnection between thought and behaviour, intention and action, and a coming apart of identity, memory and even consciousness. Sufferers may describe inappropriate or absent emotional reactions, and feeling like they are watching their lives from a distance. Particularly extreme types include dissociative amnesia and fugue, and dissociative identity disorder, which used to be known as multiple personality disorder.

Dissociative amnesia is memory loss with a psychological cause (typically dissociative disorders are brought on by stress or trauma). One of its most severe forms is fugue, a condition where the sufferer travels somewhere new and starts a new life, apparently losing or blocking out all memory of their past life, including family relations. Dissociative identity disorder is where a sufferer appears to have two or more distinct identities and switches between them, especially at times of stress.

Personality disorders with anxiety and neuroses

A diverse category of several disorders that manifest in late adolescence or early adulthood, characterized by stable and pervasive ways of thinking, and behaving and relating to other people in ways that deviate from social norms and cause distress or dysfunction.

These disorders depend greatly on social definitions; sceptics would argue they are simply medicalized labels attached to personalities and behaviours that other people do not like. Examples include:

- Borderline personality disorder, characterized by extreme emotional instability.

- Schizoid personality disorder, characterized by coldness and solitary ways.

- Antisocial personality disorder, characterized by selfish recklessness and impulsivity.

- Closely related to antisocial personality disorder is psychopathy, characterized by glib charm, lying and the lack of a conscience or empathy.

Anxiety

Severe anxiety and/or depression, with dissociation, intrusive thoughts, vivid memories, flashbacks and even hallucinations, following exposure to trauma, is known as acute stress disorder if it follows within four weeks of a traumatic event, or post-traumatic stress disorder (PTSD). It is often seen in combat veterans.

During the American Civil War, acute stress disorder was known as 'nostalgia', owing to its supposed cause, a kind

Phobias

A phobia is an irrational anxiety response to a stimulus, which may only be a representation of a real thing. For instance, ailurophobes, who are frightened of cats, may experience an anxiety response on simply seeing a photo of a cat. Common phobias include:

- Social phobia – fear of meeting people or being at social events.

- Agoraphobia – fear of crowds, public places and being away from a safe place.

- Arachnophobia – fear of spiders: this is the most common phobia in the UK, a country without poisonous spiders. Curiously in regions where there are poisonous spiders, arachnophobia is often much less common.

of homesickness. In the First World War it was called 'shell shock', and in the Second 'combat fatigue'. Only after the Vietnam War was it recognized that such stress reactions could persist long after their triggers, perhaps indefinitely. A study of 157 Second World War veterans who had been prisoners of war found that they still suffered from clinically apparent PTSD sixty-five years after the end of the war.

- Acrophobia – fear of heights, often confused with vertigo (dizziness), although this may be a symptom of acrophobia. There is evidence that elements of this are hardwired into the brain from birth. Babies who have just learned to crawl and who are tested with a 'visual cliff' – an illusion that makes it look as though they are on a cliff edge – instinctively refuse to crawl over the 'edge'.

- Carcinophobia – fear of cancer, is one of the most common examples of a phobia that can cause harm because it can prevent people from consulting their doctor, while …

- Trypanophobia – fear of injections can trigger sudden drops in blood pressure that cause fainting and can even be fatal.

Sufferers modify their behaviour to avoid triggers but even simple cues, such as weather, can trigger flashbacks.

Neurotic disorders

A neurosis is relatively milder than the anxiety, when the subject does not lose insight (i.e. is aware that they have a problem), and the condition does not have to have any biological/physiological cause. Neurosis overlaps with personality and dissociative disorders and includes anxiety -related conditions such as obsessive-compulsive disorder, eating disorders, anxiety attacks and phobias.

8

What you need to know about
HAPPINESS

If you told a friend you were going to see a psychologist, what would they say? Most likely they would be concerned, and they would probably think that you must have a problem or mental health concern. Traditionally psychology has been oriented around a disease model, and although this has led to great strides in the treatment of major illnesses such as depression and schizophrenia, it has also led to psychology being regarded in a negative light. But a growing movement in psychology, known as 'positive' or 'optimal psychology', argues that it does not have to be this way. The aim is to make seeing a psychologist akin to visiting a personal trainer.

POSITIVE PSYCHOLOGY

When the Harvard psychiatrist George E. Vaillant (b. 1934) analyzed what he called a 'standard psychiatric textbook', he found that only five lines of text out of roughly a million discussed hope and joy, and none mentioned love or compassion. This tends to obscure the fact that the roots of positive psychology go very deep into the past and the history of the study of the mind.

How to be happy was one of the guiding questions of Ancient Greek philosophy, and the views of Aristotle (384–322 BC) on what he called '*eudaimonia*' (Greek for 'happiness') would prove to have a great influence on modern positive psychology (see opposite). A quick resumé runs like this:

- When it was born in the nineteenth century, psychology attempted to move away from philosophy towards science, but even some of its earliest proponents advocated principles of positive psychology.

- William James (1842–1910), the American psychology pioneer, raised the topic of optimal psychology in his 1906 presidential address to the American Psychological Association (APA), tasking psychology with exploring the limits of 'human energy' and learning how this energy could be stimulated and put to best use. Although he pursued an objective, scientific psychology, he also advocated attending to

Aristotle and the philosophy of happiness

Aristotle believed that the guiding principle of the universe is purpose, in the sense that everything is directed towards an end or goal. The ultimate purpose of all human endeavour, the 'supreme good for man', he said, is happiness or, more specifically, living a good life in such a way that happiness results. Thus happiness is more of a process than a result, an activity rather than a state. This activity, Aristotle said, is to live in accordance with reason (the rationality of humans being their unique and essential virtue). His eudaimonic principle is to live in accordance with human virtues, pursuing activities that fully use and explore our reason. This 'good living' must inevitably lead to happiness, whatever the vicissitudes of fortune, for it is in harmony with humankind's essential nature.

the subjective experience of the individual in order to help achieve positive goals.

- The humanistic approach advanced by James was largely obscured over the following decades, with the rise of Freudian depth psychology (sometimes known as the 'First Wave' of psychology) and then the dominance of the behaviourist school (the Second Wave).

- After the Second World War the arrival of a Third Wave (or Third Force) was signalled by the work of Abraham Maslow (1908–70), an American psychologist who developed a model of human motivations known as the 'hierarchy of needs'.

- At the bottom of the hierarchy are basic biological needs, in the middle are fundamental human drives, e.g. the search for self-esteem and the need to be loved, but towards the top are 'meta' goals such as autonomy, wholeness and beauty, leading to the goal of self-actualization (becoming a fully integrated person who fulfils their potential). Beyond this are aspirations including discovery and peak experiences, and transcendence into what Maslow called the 'Z realm'. Maslow first coined the term 'positive psychology'.

- The Third Force in psychology had a profound impact on psychotherapy, helping to prompt the development of more positive, humanistic models of therapy that rejected determinism and stressed individual autonomy and the potential for growth with the pursuit of a good life. The best-known exponent of this humanistic psychology was the therapist Carl Rogers (1902–87), whose person-centred approach (also known as Rogerian therapy) was another significant influence on positive psychology.

- Positive psychology as a distinct research school is said to have been founded by the American psychologist Martin Seligman (b. 1942). When he became president of the APA he used his 1998 address to inaugurate positive psychology as a discipline, defining it as 'the scientific study of optimal human functioning that aims to discover and promote the factors that allow individuals and communities to thrive.'

Optimal psychology

Positive psychology is not simply about being happy, and indeed Seligman tries to avoid the word 'happiness' because it can mean such different things to different people. He prefers the terms 'flourishing' and 'well-being'. The goals of the movement are partly designed in opposition to the traditional disease model of psychology, so it recognizes that people want to 'thrive not just survive' and that removing 'disabling conditions' is not the same as 'building the enabling conditions that make life most worth living', and instead of trying to 'fix what's wrong' it seeks to 'build what's strong'.

Types of well-being

Positive psychology operates on three distinct levels: the subjective level, the individual level and the group level. The subjective level involves studying the subjective experience of positive emotion and activity, including joy, happiness, optimism and flow. The individual level relates to what constitutes the 'good life' and the qualities of a 'good person', looking at strengths and virtues. The group or community level relates to social and civic virtues, which enhance the well-being of communities and all their citizens.

These three levels relate to different conceptions of well-being: hedonic, eudaimonic and civic:

- Hedonic well-being is closest to the everyday understanding of 'happiness'; it includes pleasure and satisfying a desire, and can therefore be shallow, fleeting and not necessarily healthy. This concept has its roots in the writings of the ancient Greek philosopher Epicurus (341–270 BC), who reasoned that the path to a good life and well-being is to maximize pleasure and minimize pain, an approach known as the 'hedonic calculus'. But he was not simply advocating the wanton satiation of desire, as his critics contended; Epicurus pointed out that satisfying a desire could lead to pain as well as pleasure, and that the best option is to calm and neutralize desire altogether, a view with obvious parallels in Buddhism.

- Eudaimonic well-being is related to Aristotle's conception of happiness, good living and virtue. It stresses much deeper and broader visions of happiness, particularly the pursuit of virtues such as competence, excellence, generosity and compassion for their own

Culturally specific types of happiness

Positive psychology terminology, with its different types of happiness, may seem confusing. Around the world different cultures and languages have created a dizzying lexicon of terms for different types of happiness, many of them practically impossible to translate. A few examples:

- Aware – Japanese for the bittersweet enjoyment of an evanescent moment of transcendent beauty, for instance when looking at cherry blossom.

- Belum – Indonesian for 'not yet,' but with optimism that an event might yet happen.

- Magari – Italian, roughly equivalent to 'maybe' that also implies 'in my dreams' or 'if only' – a hopeful wish and wistful regret combined.

- Natsukashii – Japanese for a kind of nostalgic pleasure and yearning, blending the happiness of treasured memories with sadness for times past.

- Vorfreude – German for an exciting anticipation that comes from imagining future pleasures sake, rather than for some narrow conception of reward or personal gain.

- Civic well-being comes from 'giving back' to society, and from communities and institutions that work well and improve the well-being of their citizens and members.

Seligman's PERMA model

Ideas like these three types of well-being are integrated into Martin Seligman's PERMA model of positive psychology and human flourishing:

- **P** is is for positive emotion and relates to hedonic well-being and subjective experience, including increasing positive emotions about the past (gratitude and forgiveness), the present (mindfulness and pleasure) and the future (hope and optimism).

- **E** is for engagement and relates to concepts of flow (see page 178).

- **R** is for relationships and relates to connections with others that can produce joy, belonging, security, pride, fun and meaning, and the development of virtues such as compassion, kindness, love, altruism, etc.

- **M** is for meaning and relates to deriving a sense of meaning and purpose from transcending the individual and personal, to belong to, and serve, social and civic institutions and causes.

- **A** is for accomplishment and relates to the pursuit of virtues for their own sake, and can include anything from immersion in a hobby to excellence at sports or success at work.

Happy equals healthy?

Positive psychology can have tangible, quantifiable benefits. It can help people to perform better at work, enjoy more satisfying relationships, become more cooperative, sleep better, have greater self-control, be more resilient and be better citizens. It can also fuel stronger immune systems and better physical health, with reduced cardiovascular mortality and longer life expectancy. For example, greater enjoyment in life was associated with a 28 per cent lower risk of death, according to a 2012 study which was based on the English Longitudinal Study of Ageing, which has gathered data since 2002 on health and well-being in 11,000 men and women over the age of fifty.

PEAK EXPERIENCES AND 'FLOW'

A key concept in the field of positive psychology is flow, a kind of altered state of consciousness in which attention is completely taken up by a task or pastime, and performance is at its peak, like when athletes talk about being 'in the zone'. Like many aspects of positive psychology, it relates to older concepts, such as Freud's 'oceanic feeling' (suggesting no perceptible limits, like an ocean) and Maslow's 'peak experience' (suggesting the apex of positive sensation).

Oceanic feeling

Freud's terms describe a kind of transcendental experience, where the boundaries between the self and the rest of the universe dissolve and you feel at one with the rest of existence. In his 1930 book *Civilization and its Discontents*, Freud argued that this feeling was the mechanism behind religious experiences, and was thus behind the entire phenomenon of religion.

Freud identified the sensation 'of being one with the external world as a whole', suggesting a temporary freedom from awareness of the self and a total immersion in the environment, which would later be identified as key characteristics of 'flow consciousness'. But he confessed to struggling with the concept of oceanic feeling, both in the sense of being unable personally to access this sensation, and in the sense of it as an object of study.

'Surprised by Joy'

A very similar experience or sensation was identified by the American psychologist Abraham Maslow, a key figure in the evolution of positive psychology. Maslow had been one of the first to make happiness a central concern in his approach to psychology. In his research he encountered a phenomenon that he called the 'peak experience', perhaps because it describes the sensation of standing on top of a mountain. 'Peak experiences are sudden feelings of intense happiness and well-being,' Maslow explained; they might include 'the awareness of an 'ultimate truth' and the unity of all things'. As with oceanic feeling, the subject 'feels at one with the world' and experiences a 'loss of placing in time and space'.

Maslow argued that these experiences led to the long-term enhancement of the quality of life in all the aspects that positive psychology seeks to encourage: 'The peak-experiencer becomes more loving and more accepting, and so he becomes more spontaneous and honest and innocent', he claimed in his 1964 book *Religion, Values and Peak Experiences*. But peak experiences could not be manufactured or artificially induced, he insisted. 'In general, we are "Surprised by Joy",' he said. A peak experience could not be sought directly; it 'comes as a by-product, an epiphenomenon, for instance, of doing a fine job at a worthy task you can identify with.'

Stretched to the limit

A remarkably similar phenomenon was explored by one of the founders of positive psychology, the Hungarian-American psychologist Mihaly Csikszentmihalyi (b. 1934). Seeking the drivers of happiness through interviews with artists, musicians and sportspeople, he discovered an altered state of consciousness, which he called 'flow', and which can help lead to sensations such as Freud's oceanic feeling and Maslow's peak experience. As with these states, flow involves immersion in the environment, dissolution of psychic barriers, and the limits of time and space.

The key aspect of flow is that it is not a passive or contemplative state, but an active, engaged one. 'The best moments in our lives are not the passive, receptive, relaxing times,' Csikszentmihalyi said. 'The best moments usually occur if a person's body or mind is stretched to its limits in a voluntary effort to accomplish something difficult and worthwhile.' People in such a state described how work or productivity would seemingly 'flow' out of them, or that they were caught up in an irresistible flow. He explained flow as: 'A state in which people are so involved in an activity that nothing else seems to matter; the experience is so enjoyable that people will continue to do it ... for the sheer sake of doing it.'

The First Four Minutes

A classic example of flow comes from *The First Four Minutes*, the 1955 account by British runner Roger Bannister (1929–2018) of becoming the first to run a mile in under four minutes. Describing a transcendental experience while running, Bannister recalled that 'a fresh rhythm entered my body. No longer conscious of my movement I discovered a new unity with nature. I had found a new source of power and beauty, a source I never dreamt existed.'

Attributes of flow

Together with Jeanne Nakamura, Csikszentmihalyi set out two conditions that a task should possess in order to trigger a flow state:

- A balance between challenge and competence, so that you feel that you are taking on a challenge that will stretch you, but not to breaking point.

- Clear short-term goals or milestones, so that you can get immediate, ongoing feedback on your progress.

Nakamura and Csikszentmihalyi also set out six characteristics of the flow state. They are:

- Intense and focused concentration on what you are doing in the present moment.

- The merging of action and awareness.

- Loss of reflective self-consciousness – 'losing yourself' in the task.

- A feeling of control, so that you know you can handle whatever comes next.

- Distortion of your experience of time; usually, a sense that time has passed quickly without you noticing.

- And a sense that the experience is intrinsically rewarding – in other words, it is worth doing for its own sake, to the point where the end goal might become just an excuse for engaging in the task for the enjoyment

Flow is important both as a cause and correlate of happiness. Csikszentmihalyi sees flow states as a kind of peak experience, producing the profound and authentic contentment and satisfaction that, according to positive psychology, are characteristic of true happiness. He also views them as a natural consequence of the personality and lifestyle most strongly associated with this optimal psychology. People who are committed, creative and engaged, not in a narrow personal sense but in deeper and wider ways, with their community and their passions, are the kind of people who are truly happy.

So, one of the lessons that we can draw from optimal psychology is the importance of 'knowing yourself', which is to say exploring and understanding your own psychology and, by extension, human psychology in general. In this sense this whole book can help serve as a tool for optimizing your mental well-being, hopefully serving as a jumping off point for a fuller and deeper exploration of the myriad important and fascinating insights offered by the world of psychology.

INDEX